The Dhammapada

The
Dhammapada

A New Translation
of the Buddhist Classic
with Annotations

Gil Fronsdal

Foreword by Jack Kornfield

Shambhala
Boston & London 2006

Shambhala Publications, Inc.
Horticultural Hall
300 Massachusetts Avenue
Boston, Massachusetts 02115
www.shambhala.com

15 14 13 12 11 10 9 8

Printed in the United States of America

♾ This edition is printed on acid-free paper that meets the
American National Standards Institute Z39.48 Standard.
♻ This book is printed on 30% postconsumer recycled paper.
For more information please visit www.shambhala.com.
Distributed in the United States by Penguin Random House LLC
and in Canada by Random House of Canada Ltd

The Library of Congress catalogues the previous
edition of this book as follows:
Tipiṭaka. Suttapṭaka. Khuddakanikāya. Dhammapada. English.
The Dhammapada: a new translation of the Buddhist classic with
annotations / Gil Fronsdal; foreword by Jack Kornfield.—1st ed.
        p. cm.
Includes bibliographical references.
In English translated from Pali.
ISBN 978-1-59030-211-8 (hardcover: alk. paper)
ISBN 978-1-59030-380-1 (paperback)
1. Spiritual life—Buddhism. I. Fronsdal, Gil. II. Title.
        BQ1372.E54F76 2005
        294.3'82322—dc22
        2004023931

This translation is dedicated to my teachers

Better than reciting a hundred meaningless verses
Is one meaningful line of Dharma. (102)

Contents

CONTENTS

Foreword

You hold in your hands the most beloved of all Buddhist texts, both poetic and profound. These verses of the *Dhammapada* sum up in the simplest language the core teachings of the Buddha. Memorized and chanted by devoted followers for thousands of years, these words remind all who hear them of the universal truths expounded by the Buddha: Hatred never ends by hatred. Virtue and wise action are the foundation for happiness. And the Buddha's teachings offer the possibility of a thoroughly unshakable peace and liberation of heart for those who follow the way of the Dharma and free themselves from clinging.

This new translation is both carefully and honorably literal and beautifully modern. Through it, Gil Fronsdal, a deeply respected Western meditation teacher and Buddhist scholar, conveys in English the life of these timeless words. The *Dhammapada*'s elegant verses, many spoken by the Buddha over the long years of his teaching, were assembled by his senior monks and nuns to express his essential wisdom. Indeed, had you been there, seated under the canopy of a banyan tree, listening closely to the Buddha as he directly pointed the way for you to live a compassionate, wise, and totally free life, you might have realized enlightenment then and there.

But it is not too late. These teachings in the *Dhammapada* are as true now as the moment they were offered from the Buddha's own lips. One page, one verse alone, has the power to change your life. Do not merely read these words but take them in slowly, savor them. Let them touch your heart's deepest wisdom. Let your understanding grow. Seeing what is true, put these words into practice. Then, as the text says, let the fragrance of your virtue spread farther than the smell of rosebay and jasmine, farther than even the winds can blow. Let the practice release your heart from fear. Let the quieting of your mind and the clear seeing of the truth release you from confusion and clinging.

May these verses and the liberated and compassionate heart to which they point awaken you. May they bring you peace, wisdom, joy, and the gift of unshakable inner freedom.

May all who open this book be blessed.

Jack Kornfield
Spirit Rock Center, 2004

Preface

THE *Dhammapada* WAS FIRST INTRODUCED TO THE non-Buddhist modern world during the second half of the nineteenth century. It has come to be recognized as a great religious classic, one bearing an uncompromising message of personal self-reliance, self-mastery, and liberation.

As there are now well over fifty English translations of the *Dhammapada,* I want to explain briefly why I felt another translation was merited, and say a few words about the principles and perspectives underlying this translation.

One of the most influential English translations is by the historian of religions F. Max Müller, first published in 1870. Many succeeding "translations" are simply adaptations of Müller's work, often by people unfamiliar with Pali. Some of these are beautiful, even inspiring, but not accurate. At the same time, the language of some of the most accurate translations can be clumsy or opaque. Furthermore, the axiom that a translation mirrors the viewpoint of the translator applies to many English *Dhammapada* translations. Hindu concepts appear in English translations done in India; Theravada viewpoints have shaped translations made in such countries as Sri Lanka, Burma, and Thailand; and in the West, translations have often reflected Western viewpoints and Western preferences and interpretations of Buddhism.

A translator often has to strike a balance between literal but clumsy language and elegant but inaccurate language. I have tried to be as literal as possible while keeping the text both readable and enjoyable. Still, no one can make a completely literal translation, completely free of bias, of a text from a distant culture and a very different language. As a Western Buddhist teacher, I am acutely aware that Buddhism has been adapted and reinterpreted in the West. I believe that there is nothing inherently wrong with this tendency; indeed, it points out how Buddhism has been adapted over time and across cultures. However, I believe it is important that we be conscious of—and responsible for—just how we might be changing Buddhism. And to do this, we need to know what we are changing it from.

In this translation, I have tried to put aside my own interpretations and preferences, insofar as possible, in favor of accuracy. In attempting a literal translation, I am trying to understand early Buddhism on its own terms so I can better evaluate our modern versions of Buddhism. After nearly thirty years of practice, I remain inspired by the teachings of the Buddha, and I hope to understand better what the Buddha taught by going back to the original text and rendering it into modern English.

Although I have not been able to replicate the melodiousness and beauty of many of the Pali verses, I hope that readers will still get some sense of the poetry of the original text.

My English renderings of some Pali words may be controversial. I have tried to explain significant translation choices in the endnotes, to help the reader better understand the sense of the original. Probably the most debatable choice will be my translation of *dhamma* as "experience" in the opening two verses. Another is my choice to translate *saṃsāra* as "wandering."

One of the most difficult words to translate is the title itself, a compound made up of the words *dhamma* and *pada,* each of which has a number of meanings. *Dhamma* can mean, among other things, religious teachings, religious truth, justice, and virtue. *Pada* means "foot" and, by extension, footstep, track, path, place, and mental state. As in English, where "a foot" sometimes refers to a unit of verse, *pada* also means a line of verse, and, by extension, a saying. Besides functioning as the title of the collection, the expression *Dhammapada* occurs three times in the verses themselves. Twice I have translated it as "Dharma teaching" (verses 44–45) and the third time as "line of Dharma" (verse 102). The Sanskrit equivalent "Dharma" is used because it is in this form that the term has begun to find a place in the lexicon of the English-speaking world—see, for example, *Merriam-Webster's Collegiate Dictionary* (tenth edition)—and because left untranslated it better retains the multivalent meanings of the original. If we translate the title based on how the term *dhammapada* is used in the verses, it should probably be translated "Sayings of the Dharma," "Verses of the Dharma," or "Teachings of the Dharma." However, if we construe *pada* as "path," as in verse 21 (where *amatapada* is translated "the path to the Deathless"), the title could be "The Path of the Dharma." Ultimately, as many translators clearly concur, it may be best not to translate the title at all.

A departure from my attempts otherwise to be literal will be seen in that in some verses I have used the plural person to make the text a little more gender-neutral than the original. For the same reason, I have used male and female pronouns more or less randomly. If I had been literally faithful to the original, all personal pronouns would have been male.

It is standard convention to number the verses sequentially. I have provided this number in parentheses following each verse, with two exceptions. Sometimes verses that are paired together are numbered together. For example, for verses one and two, the numbering for both verses appears after the second verse. The other exception is where I have combined two or more closely related verses. In these cases, the verse numbers appear at the end of the combined verse. The verses have been typeset to avoid breaking any stanzas.

Every translation necessarily reflects the concerns, background, and understanding of its translator. I have been a Buddhist practitioner for nearly thirty years, including many years spent in monasteries in America, Japan, and Southeast Asia. I teach in both the Soto Zen and Theravada traditions. I received a Ph.D. in Buddhist studies from Stanford University, where my research focused on the early Indian Bodhisattva ideal. The present translation thus reflects three perspectives: that of a practitioner, seeking in the *Dhammapada* a deeper understanding of my own Buddhist practice; that of a Buddhist teacher who finds in the *Dhammapada* the inspirational words of early teachers and a useful sourcebook for teaching material; and finally that of a scholar with an appreciation of the complexities of translation and the difficulties of understanding texts across time and cultures.

Acknowledgments

IN HIS FOREWORD TO THE 1898 EDITION OF HIS English translation of the *Dhammapada*, Max Müller explains that his translation was dependent on the pioneering work of the Dutch scholar Victor Fausböll, who in 1855 had published the first translation into a Western language (Latin!). Müller writes:

> There is between a scholar such as Fausböll and the ordinary scholars who can read what has been read and translated before, about the same difference as between a Stanley exploring the darkest Africa and a tourist who now goes to Egypt personally conducted by Messrs. Cook & Co.
>
> —*The Dhammapada, Sacred Books of the East,* vol. 10, part 1, 1924, p. xii.

Max Müller and many more recent scholars laid the foundation that allowed me to translate the *Dhammapada*. I am reluctant to guess how Müller would have extended his analogy to those of us working more than a century after his time!

The English translations and studies that I found most helpful are listed in the bibliography. I am grateful to the scholars who produced them, and I would encourage anyone who is interested in further study of the *Dhammapada* to read their works.

In particular, I would like to acknowledge and offer my deep gratitude to the people who read my drafts and offered suggestions throughout the translation process. Thanissaro Bhikkhu and Professor Jan Nattier offered invaluable assistance, helping me to understand the original Pali text and to make the English translation more readable. I am also very grateful for the careful editing of the translation and the introduction done by Nancy Van House, Andrea Fella, and Barbara Gates. Angie Boisevain, Ronna Kabatznik, and Peter Dale Scott also generously read over the translations and made many helpful suggestions. Professor John Strong generously offered helpful suggestions for the introduction.

I also extend my thanks to Peter Turner, Tom Bonoma, Emily Bower, and Karen Ready at Shambhala Publications for their interest in this project and their great support in bringing it to its finished form.

I offer whatever merit that has come from producing this translation to all my teachers. May they all be happy.

Introduction

THE BUDDHA TAUGHT A PATH OF LIBERATION. To understand his teachings is to understand how to walk that path. Though he described it as an ancient pathway, hidden and forgotten until he rediscovered it, it remains as relevant today as it was in his time, twenty-five hundred years ago.

By far the most popular text teaching how to walk this path is the *Dhammapada*, a collection of verses from the earliest period of Buddhism in India. I was introduced to this sacred text when my first Zen teacher gave me my first copy. In the twenty-five years since receiving that gift, I have read and reread the *Dhammapada* many times. I have found its teachings to be direct, wise, and inspirational. The verses point to a possibility of peace and freedom that I find breathtakingly simple in its profundity.

My appreciation and understanding of the *Dhammapada* has grown over the years that I have lived with it. This has been especially true over the last four years spent translating it from Pali, the ancient Indian language in which it is preserved. In this introduction I share some of what I have learned, in the hope that this will help the contemporary English reader better appreciate the beauty and wisdom of the text.

The *Dhammapada* originated in a time, culture, and spiritual tradition very different from what is familiar to most Western readers today. We might be alerted to this difference if we compare the beginning of the *Dhammapada* with the opening lines of the Bible, which emphasize God's role as Creator and, by extension, our reliance on God's power. In contrast, the first two verses of the *Dhammapada* emphasize the power of the human mind in shaping our lives, and the importance and effectiveness of a person's own actions and choices. This theme reappears throughout the text. We are told, for example, that we are our own protectors and the shapers of our own destinies (verse 380). What we do, especially with the mind, determines our future happiness or unhappiness (verses 1–2). Each of us must make our own effort along the Buddhist path; teachers can only show the way (verse 276). Ethical and mental purity—important ideals in the *Dhammapada*—cannot be achieved through the intervention of others: "By oneself alone is one purified" (verse 165).

The *Dhammapada*, like the early Buddhist tradition, offers two distinct goals for what, in Western terms, could be called the spiritual life. The verses can frequently, even suddenly, switch to emphasize one or the other goal.

The first goal focuses on attaining happiness and welfare in this life or future lives. In future lives, a good rebirth could be as a human being in fortunate circumstances or as a heavenly being (*deva*), while a bad rebirth could be in hell (verse 126). To attain the former goal, the verses emphasize virtuous actions and basic ethical teachings. So, for example, there are teachings on living by ethical precepts (246–247), watching and disciplining one's own mind (35–36), being without hate (4), being respectful (109), avoiding evil deeds (123), being nonviolent (129–130), and curbing one's anger (231–234). Many of these are not uniquely Buddhist teachings. In fact, scholars have suggested that some verses in the *Dhammapada* may have been adapted from poetry, songs, and teachings already current in ancient India before and during the Buddha's time.

The second, ultimate, and uniquely Buddhist goal described by the *Dhammapada* is liberation. This is a form of spiritual freedom that involves a radical personal change. It consists of a purification, often described forcefully in these verses as the elimination or destruction of one's mental defilements, attachments, and hindrances. Since these mental forces keep a person bound to the cycles of rebirth, when they are overcome the practitioner is liberated from these cycles. For those who don't share the Buddhist belief in rebirth, it is hard to appreciate the central importance that Buddhism has traditionally placed in stepping off the wheel of life and death.

In line with this emphasis on purification, most of the descriptions of the ultimate goal are worded in the negative, describing what the liberated person has become freed from. So, for example, the enlightened person is free of death (86), bonds (90), conceit (94), the potential to be reborn (97), craving (154), fear (216), obsessive thinking (254), the toxins (272), suffering (354), and mental defilements (386). The more positive descriptions of the enlightened person can also be seen as descriptions of absence: such a person is someone who has gone to the Unconstructed (154) or to the immovable state (225). Even when liberation is equated with peace (96), this can perhaps be understood in terms of the absence of conflict, agitation, or suffering.

Describing the ultimate attainment by what is absent or eliminated is common in the oldest Buddhist scriptures. Sometimes this attainment is associated with "Nirvana," a word that in ancient Indian languages (e.g., Sanskrit *nirvāṇa;* Pali *nibbāna*) suggests an extinguishing or a release. I can imagine a number of reasons why positive descriptions were avoided. First, Nirvana may be indescribable in terms of our experience and language. Second, the experience of the ultimate may not be one thing. Rather, it may be like

the condition of prisoners released from prison: each
ex-prisoner shares the same freedom from incarcera-
tion, but the individual prisoners may vary widely in
how they live with that freedom.

CONTRASTING MOODS: ENERGY AND PEACE

As I became familiar with the *Dhammapada* in its original language, I noticed that, in addition to teachings,
the text also conveys two prominent moods, in keeping
with the ancient Indian theory that poetry expresses
one or another "flavor" (*rasa*) or emotional attitude. I
find that the *Dhammapada* not only awakens these
moods in me as the reader, but also helps me to feel
closer to the ancient Buddhists who composed the text.
Through the *Dhammapada* I get a sense of the emotional inspiration that early Indian Buddhists may have
had for their spiritual life.

The first mood or emotion is energetic effort (*vi-
riya*), characterized by the heroism and self-control re-
quired to walk the Buddhist path. Some verses exhort
us to action with expressions such as "Rouse yourself!
Don't be negligent! Live the Dharma" (168). The di-
rectness and crispness of many of the verses convey this
sense of energy. The spirit comes across most strongly
in the second chapter, "Vigilance," where the dharma
life is described as a purposeful life in which one ac-
tively cultivates a high degree of self-mastery.

The second prominent "flavor" expressed in the *Dhammapada* is the state of peace (*santi*) that comes with the fulfillment of the path of practice. At times the text explicitly contrasts this with the effortful activity of someone still on the path (e.g., verse 23). Associated with this peace are tranquillity, rest, purity, happiness, and freedom. The chapters that most clearly express the peace and its associated qualities are chapters 15 and 25.

THEMES

Many of the important themes found in the *Dhammapada* are presented as dichotomies: for example, being vigilant versus being negligent, having self-control or not having it, having ill will and not having it, being truthful or not, developing the mind or not developing it, grief versus joy. Even the poetic structure of the *Dhammapada* is often built around dichotomies. Many verses are paired to present the two sides of a distinction. This is most pronounced in the first chapter, appropriately titled "Dichotomies." Some pairs of chapters seem to represent dichotomies as well, for example a chapter on "The Fool" followed by one on "The Sage."

In other texts, this characteristic might be of only casual interest. In the *Dhammapada,* however, it is a manifestation of how important simple distinctions are in the pragmatism of the early Buddhist tradition. What matters is whether something does or does not work, is or is not helpful in the spiritual quest. All the dichotomies in the *Dhammapada* can be seen as extensions of this simple pragmatic concern. One of the most explicit expressions of this tendency is found in verse 282, which focuses on the distinction between what increases or decreases a person's wisdom:

> *Wisdom arises from [spiritual] practice;*
> > *Without practice it decays.*
> *Knowing this two-way path for gain and loss,*
> > *Conduct yourself so that wisdom grows.*

A common dichotomy in the text is the contrast between action that is meritorious and that which I have mostly translated as "evil." "Merit" is a relatively unproblematic translation of *puñña*; certainly it is preferable to "good," as the word is sometimes translated. I have used "evil" to translate *pāpa*. The concept is perhaps closer to "demerit" (as I translated it in verse 39), but I felt that word was usually too mild. *Pāpa* is what causes suffering in oneself as well as harm to other people. It is the causal condition for an unfortunate rebirth (117–118).

The theme of evil also appears in recurring references to Māra. A person bent on liberation needs to battle Māra (40), avoid being overpowered by him

(7–8), and ultimately conquer him (175). Western readers sometimes see Māra as the Buddhist version of the devil, especially when he is called *pāpimā*, "the Evil One." But because *pāpa* relates to demeritorious action, *pāpimā* could perhaps be understood as one who pulls people downward in the cycles of rebirth. The word *Māra*, derived from the verbal root *mṛ*, "to die," refers to that which kills. Verses that speak of not being seen by Māra (e.g., 46, 170) mean, I suggest, that one overcomes death. This does not mean that liberated people don't die. Rather, it suggests first, that the person is no longer susceptible to the deadening forces of Māra, such as fear, anger, and clinging; and second, that a liberated person is free from the forces leading to further rebirth and thus to further death.

Another common contrast in the text is between the wise person and the fool, or perhaps between the wise person and a childish one; *bāla,* the fool, also means "child" or "childish." The fool acts in ways harmful to him or herself; a wise person, in ways that are beneficial. Furthermore, the wise person clearly sees these dichotomies:

> *Not by silence*
> > *Does an ignorant fool become a sage.*
> *The wise person, who,*
> > *As if holding a set of scales,*
> *Selects what's good and avoids what's evil*
> > *Is, for that reason, a sage.*

*Whoever can weigh these two sides of the
    world
  Is, for that reason, called a "sage."*
  (268–269)

Such verses can come across as judgmental and lacking compassion. However, I believe that the purpose is not to denigrate some people as fools, but rather to describe the difference between skillful and unskillful behavior, between what leads to desirable outcomes and what does not. Fools are sometimes presented as people who are evil, but more often as people who are oblivious or distracted by worldly attachments (see, e.g., 286–287).

ON READING THE *Dhammapada*

During many years of reading the *Dhammapada*, I have spent a lot of time pondering two issues related to the text and their meaning for the modern lay practitioner: first, the emphasis on renunciation, solitude, and the monastic life; and second, what may appear to be a denial or rejection of the world.

The major audience for the *Dhammapada* historically has been the ordained Buddhist community. Thus a number of the verses understandably address issues of monastic life. However, many of these verses can apply to anyone who seeks a life dedicated to dharma practice. The challenge for lay practitioners is to discover how to appropriately incorporate into lay life the renunciation and purity that characterize monastic life. I have taken them that way for myself. When verses 9 and 10 state that the monastic form is useless unless the monk or nun is virtuous, self-controlled, and honest, I translate that for myself as saying that the lay life is similarly worthless without these qualities. Anyone who lives in this way may figuratively be called a monastic, as is done in verse 142.

The second issue—whether the text has a world-rejecting message—is more challenging, perhaps because the text was meant to challenge our relationship to the world. An initial reading of a number of the verses seems to reveal a negation or an aversion to the world (in fact, some English translations seem to translate the entire text based on this impression). For example, the text encourages us not to "be engrossed in the world" (167). Certainly, for many readers, the following verse seems to deny ordinary human relationships:

> *Affection gives rise to grief;*
> *Affection gives rise to fear.*
> *For someone released from affection*
> *There is no grief;*
> *And from where would come fear? (213)*

However, if affection is here understood as a form of clinging—which I believe was the original intent—then what is being criticized is not warm or caring relationships but clinging to those relationships. Similarly, it is not the world that is negated in the *Dhammapada,* but rather *attachment* to the world (as in verse 171).

Stated differently, what is rejected in the text is *saṃsāra,* the self-perpetuating cycles of suffering arising from clinging. Becoming free from wandering endlessly in these cycles is the essential goal of the *Dhammapada.* The world and *saṃsāra* are not the same, even though it is the world that provides most of the objects of samsaric clinging.

In contrast to the seemingly world-negating verses, the *Dhammapada* places a strong emphasis on joy, with an entire section, chapter 15, devoted to happiness. Here we find many expressions of joy, including exclamations of joy from those who have freed themselves from attachments. They say, "We shall feast on joy" (200).

For these reasons, I have come to understand that the overall message is not to avoid the world, but rather to avoid being attached. While initial appearances may sometimes suggest a world-negating message, I believe that the issue in the *Dhammapada* is neither negating or affirming the world. The issue is becoming free of clinging to the world. For those who take on this challenge, the resulting freedom helps us live in the world as wisely as possible, which includes experiencing joy.

Over the years I have read the *Dhammapada* in a variety of ways, sometimes casually and sometimes with great care. I have calmed my mind in meditation so that I could encounter the text in creative and intuitive ways. I have read it out loud. I have memorized verses. Some passages I have reread many times until they revealed new understandings or insights. I have read the verses for my own inspiration as well as to discover what inspired ancient Buddhists in their religious life. At times I have approached the text with an inquiring attitude, sometimes to see how the text might address a particular question I've had and sometimes to allow the text to question my own views and biases.

Each way of reading the text gives me a different impression of the *Dhammapada*. Using a variety of approaches has enriched my experience of the text. My hope is that my translation will enable other readers to be enriched by it as well, perhaps showing them something of the happiness toward which this religious classic is a guide.

The Dhammapada

ONE

Dichotomies*

All experience is preceded by mind,
    Led by mind,
    Made by mind.
Speak or act with a corrupted mind,
    And suffering follows
As the wagon wheel follows the hoof of the ox.

All experience is preceded by mind,
    Led by mind,
    Made by mind.
Speak or act with a peaceful mind,
    And happiness follows
Like a never-departing shadow.   (1–2)*

---

* An asterisk indicates an associated endnote of explanation or
  elaboration.

"He abused me, attacked me,
        Defeated me, robbed me!"
For those carrying on like this,
        Hatred does not end.

"She abused me, attacked me,
        Defeated me, robbed me!"
For those not carrying on like this,
        Hatred ends.   (3–4)

Hatred never ends through hatred.
        By non-hate alone does it end.
        This is an ancient truth.

Many do not realize that
        We here must die.
        For those who realize this,
        Quarrels end.   (5–6)*

Whoever lives
        Focused on the pleasant,
        Senses unguarded,
        Immoderate with food,
        Lazy and sluggish,
Will be overpowered by Māra,
        As a weak tree is bent in the wind.

Whoever lives
>   Focused on the unpleasant,
>   Senses guarded,
>   Moderate with food,
>   Faithful and diligent,
Will not be overpowered by Māra,
>   As a stone mountain is unmoved by the wind.

(7–8)*

Whoever is defiled
>   And devoid of self-control and truth,
>   Yet wears the saffron robe,
Is unworthy of the saffron robe.

Whoever has purged the defilements,
>   Is self-controlled, truthful,
>   And well established in virtue,
Is worthy of the saffron robe.   (9–10)*

Those who consider the inessential to be essential
>   And see the essential as inessential
Don't reach the essential,
>   Living in the field of wrong intention.

Those who know the essential to be essential
>   And the inessential as inessential
Reach the essential,
>   Living in the field of right intention.   (11–12)*

As rain penetrates
      An ill-thatched house,
So lust penetrates
      An uncultivated mind.

As rain does not penetrate
      A well-thatched house,
So lust does not penetrate
      A well-cultivated mind.   (13–14)*

One who does evil grieves in this life,
      Grieves in the next,
      Grieves in both worlds.
Seeing one's own defiled acts brings grief and affliction.

One who makes merit rejoices in this life,
      Rejoices in the next,
      Rejoices in both worlds.
Seeing one's own pure acts brings joy and delight.

                                    (15–16)

One who does evil is tormented in this life,
      Tormented in the next,
      Is tormented in both worlds.
Here he is tormented, knowing, "I have done evil."
      Reborn in realms of woe, he is tormented all the
         more.

4

One who makes merit is delighted in this life,
    Delighted in the next,
    Is delighted in both worlds.
Here she is delighted, knowing, "I have made merit."
    Reborn in realms of bliss, she delights all the
        more.   (17–18)*

One who recites many teachings
    But, being negligent, doesn't act accordingly,
    Like a cowherd counting others' cows,
Does not attain the benefits of the contemplative life.

One who recites but a few teachings
    Yet lives according to the Dharma,
    Abandoning passion, ill will, and delusion,
    Aware and with mind well freed,
    Not clinging in this life or the next,
Attains the benefits of the contemplative life.   (19–20)

5

TWO

Vigilance*

Vigilance is the path to the Deathless;
    Negligence the path to death.
The vigilant do not die;
    The negligent are as if already dead.   (21)*

Knowing this distinction,
    Vigilant sages rejoice in vigilance
Delighting
    In the field of the noble ones.   (22)*

Absorbed in meditation, persevering,
    Always steadfast,
The wise touch Nirvana,
    The ultimate rest from toil.   (23)*

Glory grows for a person who is
        Energetic and mindful,
        Pure and considerate in action,
        Restrained and vigilant,
        And who lives the Dharma.   (24)

Through effort, vigilance,
        Restraint, and self-control,
The wise person can become an island
        No flood will overwhelm.   (25)*

Unwise, foolish people
        Give themselves over to negligence.
The wise
        Protect vigilance as the greatest treasure. (26)

Don't give yourself to negligence,
        Don't devote yourself to sensual pleasure.
Vigilant and absorbed in meditation
        One attains abundant happiness.   (27)

Driving away negligence with vigilance,
        Ascending the tower of insight and free of sorrow,
A sage observes the sorrowing masses
        As someone standing on a mountain observes
                fools on the ground below.   (28)

Vigilant among the negligent,
    Wide awake among the sleeping,
The wise one advances
    Like a swift horse leaving a weak one behind.

           (29)

With vigilance, Indra became the greatest of the gods.
    The gods praise vigilance,
    Forever rejecting negligence.   (30)*

The monastic who delights in vigilance
    And fears negligence
    Advances like a fire,
    Burning fetters subtle and gross.   (31)

The monastic who delights in vigilance
    And fears negligence
    Is incapable of backsliding
    And is quite close to Nirvana.   (32)

THREE

The Mind

The restless, agitated mind,
	Hard to protect, hard to control,
The sage makes straight,
	As a fletcher the shaft of an arrow. (33)

Like a fish out of water,
	Thrown on dry ground,
This mind thrashes about,
	Trying to escape Māra's command. (34)

The mind, hard to control,
	Flighty—alighting where it wishes—
One does well to tame.
	The disciplined mind brings happiness. (35)

The mind, hard to see,
Subtle—alighting where it wishes—
The sage protects.
The watched mind brings happiness. (36)

Far-ranging, solitary,
Incorporeal and hidden
Is the mind.
Those who restrain it
Will be freed from Māra's bonds. (37)*

For those who are unsteady of mind,
Who do not know true Dharma,
And whose serenity wavers,
Wisdom does not mature. (38)

For one who is awake,
Whose mind isn't overflowing,
Whose heart isn't afflicted
And who has abandoned both merit and demerit,
Fear does not exist. (39)*

Knowing this body to be like a clay pot,
Establishing this mind like a fortress,
One should battle Māra with the sword of insight,
Protecting what has been won,
Clinging to nothing. (40)*

All too soon this body
        Will lie on the ground,
Cast aside, deprived of consciousness,
        Like a useless scrap of wood.   (41)

Whatever an enemy may do to an enemy,
        Or haters, one to another,
Far worse is the harm
        From one's own wrongly directed mind.   (42)*

Neither mother nor father,
        Nor any other relative can do
One as much good
        As one's own well-directed mind.   (43)

FOUR

Flowers

Who will master this world
    And the realms of Yama and the gods?
Who will select a well-taught Dharma teaching,
    As a skilled person selects a flower?   (44)*

One in training will master this world
    And the realms of Yama and the gods.
One in training will select
    A well-taught Dharma teaching,
    As a skilled person selects a flower.   (45)*

Knowing this body is like foam,
    Fully awake to its mirage-like nature,
Cutting off Māra's flowers,
    One goes unseen by the King of Death.   (46)

Death sweeps away
    The person obsessed
With gathering flowers,
    As a great flood sweeps away a sleeping village.

(47)*

The person obsessed
    With gathering flowers,
Insatiable for sense pleasures,
    Is under the sway of Death.   (48)*

As a bee gathers nectar
    And moves on without harming
    The flower, its color, or its fragrance,
Just so should a sage walk through a village.   (49)

Do not consider the faults of others
    Or what they have or haven't done.
Consider rather
    What you yourself have or haven't done.   (50)

Like a beautiful flower,
    Brightly colored but lacking scent,
So are well-spoken words
    Fruitless when not carried out.

Like a beautiful flower,
    Brightly colored and with scent,
So are well-spoken words
    Fruitful when carried out.   (51–52)

Just as from a heap of flowers
    Many garlands can be made,
So, you, with your mortal life,
    Should do many skillful things.   (53)

The scent of flowers
    —sandalwood, jasmine, and rosebay—
    Doesn't go against the wind.
But the scent of a virtuous person
    Does travel against the wind;
    It spreads in all directions.   (54)*

The scent of virtue
    Is unsurpassed
Even by sandalwood, rosebay,
    Water lily, and jasmine.   (55)

Slight
    Is the scent of rosebay or sandalwood,
But the scent of the virtuous is supreme,
    Drifting even to the gods.   (56)

Māra does not find the path
    Of those endowed with virtue,
Living with vigilance,
    and freed by right understanding.   (57)

As a sweet-smelling lotus
    Pleasing to the heart
    May grow in a heap of rubbish
    Discarded along the highway,
So a disciple of the Fully Awakened One
    Shines with wisdom
    Amid the rubbish heap
    Of blind, common people.   (58–59)*

FIVE

The Fool*

Night is long for one lying awake.
Seven miles is long for one exhausted.
Samsara is long for fools
    Ignorant of true Dharma.   (60)

If, while on your way,
    You meet no one your equal or better,
Steadily continue on your way alone.
    There is no fellowship with fools.   (61)

A fool suffers, thinking,
    "I have children! I have wealth!"
One's self is not even one's own.
    How then are children? How then is wealth?

                                                    (62)

A fool conscious of her foolishness
    Is to that extent wise.
But a fool who considers himself wise
    Is the one to be called a fool.   (63)

A fool associating with a sage,
    Even if for a lifetime,
Will no more perceive the Dharma
    Than a spoon will perceive the taste of soup.

        (64)

A discerning person who associates with a sage,
    Even if for a brief moment,
Will quickly perceive the Dharma,
    As the tongue perceives the taste of soup.   (65)

Fools with no sense
    Go about as their own enemies,
Doing evil deeds that
    Bear bitter fruit.   (66)

No deed is good
    That one regrets having done,
    That results in weeping
    And a tear-streaked face.   (67)

A deed is good
>That one doesn't regret having done,
>That results in joy
>And delight. (68)

As long as evil has not borne fruit,
>The fool thinks it is like honey.
But when evil does bear fruit,
>Then the fool suffers. (69)

The foolish ascetic who month after month
>Eats food with the tip of a blade of grass
Is not worth a fraction
>Of a person who has fathomed the Dharma.

(70)*

Like fresh milk,
>Evil deeds do not immediately curdle;
Rather, like fire covered with ash,
>They follow the fool, smoldering. (71)*

Reasoning is harmful
>To fools;
It ruins their good fortune
>And splits open their heads. (72)*

Fools will want unwarranted status,
  Deference from fellow monks,
Authority in the monasteries,
  And homage from good families.
"Let both householders and renunciants
  Believe that *I* did *this*.
  Let them obey me in every task!"
Such are the thoughts of a fool
  Who cultivates desire and pride.   (73–74)

The way to material gain is one thing,
  The path to Nirvana another.
Knowing this, a monk who is the Buddha's disciple
  Should not delight in being venerated,
  But cultivate solitude instead.   (75)*

SIX

The Sage

Like someone pointing to treasure
    Is the wise person
Who sees your faults and points them out.
    Associate with such a sage.
Good will come of it, not bad,
    If you associate with one such as this.   (76)

Let one such as this advise you, instruct you,
    And restrain you from rude behavior.
Such a person is pleasing to good people,
    But displeasing to the bad.   (77)

Do not associate with evil friends;
    Do not associate with the lowest of people.
Associate with virtuous friends;
    Associate with the best of people.   (78)

One who drinks in the Dharma
      Sleeps happily with a clear mind.
The sage always delights in the Dharma
      Taught by the noble ones.   (79)*

Irrigators guide water;
      Fletchers shape arrows;
Carpenters fashion wood;
      Sages tame themselves.   (80)

As a solid mass of rock
      Is not moved by the wind,
So a sage is unmoved
      By praise or blame.   (81)

As a deep lake
      Is clear and undisturbed,
So a sage becomes clear
      Upon hearing the Dharma.   (82)

Virtuous people always let go.
      They don't prattle about pleasures and desires.
Touched by happiness and then by suffering,
      The sage shows no sign of being elated or
         depressed.   (83)*

A person who would not wish for success by unethical
    means,
        Not for the sake of oneself,
        Not for the sake of others,
        Not with hopes for children, wealth, or kingdom,
Is a person of virtue, insight, and truth.   (84)*

Few are the people
    Who reach the other shore.
Many are the people
    Who run about on this shore.   (85)

But those who are in accord with the Dharma
    —with the well-taught Dharma—
Will go beyond the realm of Death,
    So hard to cross.   (86)

Giving up dark ways,
    Sages cultivate the bright.
They go from home to homelessness,
    To the solitude so hard to enjoy.

There they should seek delight,
    Abandoning sensual desires,
    Having nothing.
Sages should cleanse themselves
    Of what defiles the mind.   (87–88)*

Those who
> Fully cultivate the Factors of Awakening,
> Give up grasping,
> Enjoy non-clinging,
> And have destroyed the toxins,

Are luminous,
And completely liberated in this life.   (89)*

SEVEN

The Arahant

For someone
    At the journey's end,
    Freed of sorrow,
    Liberated in all ways,
    Released from all bonds,
No fever exists. (90)*

The mindful apply themselves;
    They don't amuse themselves in any abode.
Like swans flying from a lake,
    They abandon home after home. (91)

Like the path of birds in the sky,
     It is hard to trace the path
Of those who do not hoard,
     Who are judicious with their food,
And whose field
     Is the freedom of emptiness and signlessness.

(92)*

Like the path of birds in the sky,
     It is hard to trace the path
Of those who have destroyed their toxins,
     Who are unattached to food,
And whose field
     Is the freedom of emptiness and signlessness.

(93)*

Even the gods cherish
     Those who are without toxins,
Who have abandoned conceit,
     And whose senses are calm,
Like horses well tamed by a charioteer.   (94)

For a person
     Who, like the earth, is untroubled,
     Who is well-practiced,
     Who is like a pillar of Indra,
     Who is like a lake without mud,
There is no more wandering.   (95)*

Calm in mind, speech, and action
    And released through right understanding,
Such a person
    Is fully at peace.   (96)

The person who
    Has gone beyond faith,
    Knows the Unmade,
    Has severed the link,
    Destroyed the potential [for rebirth],
    And eliminated clinging
Is the ultimate person.   (97)*

In village, in forest,
    In low land, in high land:
Delightful is the place
    Where the arahant dwells.   (98)

Delightful are forests
    Where the public does not delight.
There the passion-free delight,
    Not seeking sensual pleasure.   (99)

EIGHT

Thousands

Better than a thousand meaningless statements
  Is one meaningful word,
Which, having been heard,
  Brings peace.   (100)

Better than a thousand meaningless verses
  Is one meaningful line of verse
Which, having been heard,
  Brings peace.   (101)

Better than reciting a hundred meaningless verses
  Is one line of Dharma
Which, having been heard,
  Brings peace.   (102)*

Greater in combat
    Than a person who conquers
A thousand times a thousand people
    Is the person who conquers herself.   (103)

Certainly it is better to conquer
    Oneself than others.
For someone who is self-restrained
    And always lives with mastery,
Neither a god, a *gandhabba,*
    Nor Mārā and Brahmā together
Could turn conquest into defeat.   (104–105)*

Better than a thousand ritual sacrifices
    Offered every month for a hundred years
Is one moment's homage offered
    To one who has cultivated herself.   (106)

Better than a hundred years
    In the forest tending a ritual fire
Is one moment's homage offered
    To one who has cultivated himself.   (107)

Whatever sacrifice or offering a merit seeker
    Might perform in an entire year
Is not worth one-fourth as much as
    Expressing respect to those who are upright.

    (108)

For the person who shows respect
    And always reveres worthy people,
Four things increase:
    Life span, beauty, happiness, and strength.   (109)

Better than one hundred years lived
    With an unsettled [mind],
    Devoid of virtue,
Is one day lived
    Virtuous and absorbed in meditation.   (110)*

Better than one hundred years lived
    With an unsettled [mind],
    Devoid of insight,
Is one day lived
    With insight and absorbed in meditation.   (111)*

Better than one hundred years lived
    Lazily and lacking in effort
Is one day lived
    With vigor and exertion.   (112)

Better than one hundred years lived
    Without seeing the arising and passing of things
Is one day lived
    Seeing their arising and passing.   (113)*

Better than one hundred years lived
    Without seeing the Deathless
Is one day lived
    Seeing the Deathless. (114)*

Better than one hundred years lived
    Without seeing the ultimate Dharma
Is one day lived
    Seeing the ultimate Dharma. (115)

NINE

Evil

Be quick to do good,
    Restrain your mind from evil.
When one is slow to make merit,
    One's mind delights in evil.   (116)

Having done something evil,
    Don't repeat it,
    Don't wish for it:
Evil piled up brings suffering.   (117)

Having done something meritorious,
    Repeat it,
    Wish for it:
Merit piled up brings happiness.   (118)

Even an evildoer may see benefit
      As long as the evil
      Has yet to mature.
But when the evil has matured,
      The evildoer
      Will meet with misfortune.   (119)*

A doer of good may meet evil fortune
      As long as the good
      Has yet to mature.
But when the good has matured,
      The doer of good
      Will meet with good fortune.   (120)

Don't disregard evil, thinking,
      "It won't come back to me!"
With dripping drops of water
      Even a water jug is filled.
Little by little,
      A fool is filled with evil.   (121)

Don't disregard merit, thinking,
      "It won't come back to me!"
With dripping drops of water
      Even a water jug is filled.
Little by little,
      A sage is filled with merit.   (122)

As a merchant
    Carrying great wealth in a small caravan
    Avoids a dangerous road;
As someone who loves life
    Avoids poison;
So should you avoid evil deeds.   (123)

A hand that has no wounds
    Can carry poison;
Poison does not enter without a wound.
    There are no evil consequences
For one who does no evil.   (124)*

Like fine dust thrown against the wind,
    Evil comes back to the fool
Who harms a person who is
    Innocent, pure, and unblemished.   (125)

Some are reborn in a womb;
Evildoers are reborn in hell.
People of good conduct go to heaven;
Those without toxins
    Are fully released in Nirvana.   (126)

You will not find a spot in the world—
    Not in the sky, not in the ocean,
    Not inside a mountain cave—
Where you will be free from your evil karma.   (127)

You will not find a spot in the world—
    Not in the sky, not in the ocean,
    Not inside a mountain cave—
Where death will not overtake you.   (128)

TEN

Violence*

All tremble at violence;
    All fear death.
Seeing others as being like yourself,
    Do not kill or cause others to kill.   (129)*

All tremble at violence;
    Life is dear for all.
Seeing others as being like yourself,
    Do not kill or cause others to kill.   (130)*

If, desiring happiness,
    You use violence
To harm living beings who desire happiness,
    You won't find happiness after death.   (131)

If, desiring happiness,
 You do not use violence
To harm living beings who desire happiness,
 You will find happiness after death.   (132)

Don't speak harshly to anyone;
 What you say will be said back to you.
Hostile speech is painful,
 And you will meet with retaliation.   (133)

If, like a broken bell,
 You do not reverberate,
Then you have attained Nirvana
 And no hostility is found in you.   (134)

As, with a stick, a cowherd drives
 Cows to pasture,
So aging and death drive
 The lives of beings.   (135)

Even while doing evil,
 Fools are ignorant of it.
Like someone burned by fire,
 Those lacking wisdom are scorched by their own
  deeds.   (136)

Whoever uses violence to harm
    The nonviolent and innocent
Quickly goes to one of ten conditions:
    Intense pain or great loss,
    Bodily injury or insanity,
    Serious illness or vicious slander,
    Oppression from rulers or the loss of relatives,
    Houses consumed by fire or wealth destroyed.
And with the breakup of the body
    The unwise one falls to hell.   (137–140)

No nakedness or matted hair,
    No filth, dust, or dirt,
No fasting or sleeping on bare ground,
    No austerities in a squatting posture
Purify a mortal who has not overcome doubt.   (141)

Even though well adorned,
    If one lives at peace,
Calmed, controlled, assured, and chaste,
    Having given up violence toward all beings,
Then one is a brahmin, a renunciant, a monastic.

    (142)*

Where in this world does one find
    Someone restrained by conscience,
    Who knows little of blame,
    As a good horse knows little of the whip?   (143)*

Like a good horse alert to the whip,
    Be ardent and alarmed.
With faith, virtue, effort,
    Concentration, and discernment,
Accomplished in knowledge and good conduct,
    Mindful,
You will leave this great suffering behind.   (144)*

Irrigators guide water;
    Fletchers shape arrows;
Carpenters fashion wood;
    The well-practiced tame themselves.   (145)

ELEVEN

Old Age

Why the laughter, why the joy,
    When flames are ever burning?
Surrounded by darkness,
    Shouldn't you search for light?   (146)

Look at this beautified body:
    A mass of sores propped up,
    Full of illness, [the object] of many plans,
    With nothing stable or lasting.   (147)*

This body is worn out—
    So fragile, a nesting ground for disease.
When life ends in death,
    This putrid body dissolves.   (148)*

What is the delight
        In seeing these dull-white bones
Tossed away
        Like white gourds in autumn?   (149)

This city is built of bones,
        Plastered with blood and flesh,
And filled with
        Aging, death, conceit, and hypocrisy.   (150)

Even the splendid chariots of the royalty wear out.
        So too does the body decay.
But the Dharma of the virtuous doesn't decay
        [For it is upheld when] the virtuous teach [it] to
                good people.   (151)*

The person of little learning
        Grows old like an ox:
The flesh increases,
        But insight does not.   (152)

Through many births
        I have wandered on and on,
Searching for, but never finding,
        The builder of [this] house.
To be born again and again is suffering.

House-builder, you are seen!
        You will not build a house again!
All the rafters are broken,
        The ridgepole destroyed;
The mind, gone to the Unconstructed,
        Has reached the end of craving!   (153–154)*

Those who have neither lived the chaste life
        Nor gained wealth in their youth
Waste away like frail herons
        In a lake devoid of fish.   (155)*

Those who have neither lived the chaste life
        Nor gained wealth in their youth
Lie around like [arrows misfired] from a bow,
        Lamenting the past.   (156)

TWELVE

Oneself

If one knew oneself to be precious,
  One would guard oneself with care.
The sage will watch over herself
  In any part
  Of the night.   (157)*

In first establishing himself
  In what is proper
And only then teaching others,
  The sage will not be stained.   (158)

As one instructs others,
  So should one do oneself:
Only the self-controlled should restrain others.
  Truly, it's hard to restrain oneself. (159)

Oneself, indeed, is one's own protector.
    What other protector could there be?
With self-control
    One gains a protector hard to obtain.   (160)

By oneself alone is evil done.
    Born of oneself, produced by oneself,
It grinds down those devoid of wisdom,
    As a diamond grinds down a gem.   (161)

They who cover themselves with their own corrupt
    conduct,
    Like a creeper covers a tree,
Do to themselves
    What an enemy wishes for them.   (162)

It's easy to do what is not good
    And things that harm oneself.
It's very difficult to do
    Things beneficial and good.   (163)

The unwise who rely on evil views
    To malign the teachings of the noble arahants
        Who live the Dharma
Produce fruit that destroys themselves,
    Like the *kathaka* reed that dies upon bearing
        fruit.   (164)*

Evil is done by oneself alone;
    By oneself is one defiled.
Evil is avoided by oneself;
    By oneself alone is one purified.
Purity and impurity depend on oneself;
    No one can purify another.   (165)

Don't give up your own welfare
    For the sake of others' welfare, however great.
Clearly know your own welfare
    And be intent on the highest good.   (166)

THIRTEEN

The World

Do not follow an inferior way;
    Don't live with negligence.
Do not follow a wrong view;
    Don't be engrossed in the world.   (167)*

Rouse yourself! Don't be negligent!
    Live the Dharma, a life of good conduct.
One who lives the Dharma is happy
    In this world and the next.   (168)

Live the Dharma, a life of good conduct.
Don't live a life of bad conduct.
One who lives the Dharma is happy
    In this world and the next.   (169)

If one sees the world as a bubble,
    If one sees it as a mirage,
One won't be seen
    By the King of Death. (170)

Come, look on this world
    As a beautified royal chariot.
Fools flounder in it,
    But the discerning do not cling. (171)

Whoever recovers from doing evil
    By doing something wholesome
Illuminates the world
    Like the moon set free from a cloud. (172)

Whoever replaces an evil deed
    With what is wholesome
Illuminates the world
    Like the moon set free from a cloud. (173)*

Blind is this world;
    Few see clearly here.
As birds who escape from nets are few,
    Few go to heaven. (174)

Swans travel the path of the sun;
    Those with psychic powers travel through space;
The wise travel forth from the world,
    Having conquered Māra and his army.   (175)*

For people who speak falsely,
    Who transgress in this one way,
    And who reject the world beyond,
There is no evil they won't do.   (176)*

Fools don't praise generosity;
    Misers don't go to the world of gods.
The wise rejoice in generosity
    And so find happiness in the hereafter.   (177)

Absolute rule over the earth,
    Going to heaven,
Supreme sovereignty over all worlds—
    The fruit of stream entry surpasses them all.

        (178)*

FOURTEEN

The Buddha*

The Buddha's victory cannot be undone;
    No one in the world can approach it.
By what path would you guide him,
    Who has no path,
    Whose field is endless?   (179)

The Buddha has no ensnaring, embroiling craving
    To lead him;
By what path would you guide him,
    Who has no path,
    Whose field is endless?   (180)

Even the gods envy
    The awakened ones,
    The mindful ones,
    The wise ones
Who are intent on meditation
    And delight in the peace of renunciation.   (181)

It is difficult to be born a human;
    Difficult is the life of mortals;
It is difficult to hear the true Dharma;
    Difficult is the arising of buddhas.   (182)

Doing no evil,
    Engaging in what's skillful,
And purifying one's mind:
    This is the teaching of the buddhas.   (183)

Patient endurance is the supreme austerity.
    The buddhas say that Nirvana is supreme.
One who injures others is no renunciant;
    One who harms another is no contemplative.

                                                   (184)*

Not disparaging others, not causing injury,
Practicing restraint by the monastic rules,
Knowing moderation in food,
Dwelling in solitude,
And pursuing the higher states of mind,
    This is the teaching of the buddhas.   (185)

Not even with a shower of gold coins
    Would we find satisfaction in sensual craving.
Knowing that sensual cravings are suffering,
    That they bring little delight,
The sage does not rejoice
    Even in divine pleasures.
One who delights in the ending of craving
    Is a disciple of the Fully Awakened One. (186–187)

People threatened by fear
    Go to many refuges:
To mountains, forests,
    Parks, trees, and shrines.
None of these is a secure refuge;
    None is a supreme refuge.
Not by going to such a refuge
    Is one released from all suffering. (188–189)

But when someone going for refuge
    To the Buddha, Dharma, and Sangha
Sees, with right insight,
    The Four Noble Truths:
        Suffering,
        The arising of suffering,
        The overcoming of suffering,
        And the Eightfold Path
        Leading to the ending of suffering,
Then this is the secure refuge;
    This is the supreme refuge.
By going to such a refuge
    One is released from all suffering.   (190–192)*

It's hard to find a noble person;
    Such a person is not born everywhere.
When such a wise one is born,
    The family flourishes in happiness.   (193)

Happy is the arising of buddhas;
    Happy is the teaching of the true Dharma;
Happy is the harmony of the Sangha;
    Happy is the ardent practice of those in harmony.

    (194)*

The merit of worshipping those worthy of worship,
    Be they buddhas or disciples
        Who have transcended their obsessive
           thinking,
        Passed beyond sorrow and grief,
        Gone to peace,
        And who have nothing to fear,
Can never be calculated by any estimation.   (195–196)*

FIFTEEN

Happiness

Ah, so happily we live,
   Without hate among those with hate.
Among people who hate
   We live without hate.   (197)*

Ah, so happily we live,
   Without misery among those in misery.
Among people in misery
   We live without misery.   (198)

Ah, so happily we live,
   Without ambition among those with ambition.
Among people who are ambitious
   We live without ambition.   (199)*

Ah, so happily we live,
  We who have no attachments.
We shall feast on joy,
  As do the Radiant Gods.   (200)*

Victory gives birth to hate;
  The defeated sleep in anguish.
Giving up both victory and defeat,
  Those who have attained peace sleep happily.

   (201)

There is no fire like lust,
  No misfortune like hate,
No suffering like the aggregates,
  And no happiness higher than peace. (202)*

Hunger is the foremost illness;
  Saṅkhāras the foremost suffering.
For one who knows this as it really is,
  Nirvana is the foremost happiness. (203)*

Health is the foremost possession,
  Contentment, the foremost wealth,
Trust, the foremost kinship,
  And Nirvana, the foremost happiness. (204)

Tasting the flavor
      Of solitude and peace,
One becomes free of distress and evil,
      Drinking the flavor of Dharma joy.   (205)

It's good to see the noble ones;
      Their company is always a delight.
Free from the sight of fools,
      One would constantly be happy.   (206)

One who keeps company with fools
      Will grieve for a long, long time.
Living with fools is painful,
      As is living with foes.
Living with the wise is delightful,
      Like relatives gathered together.   (207)

Therefore:
You should follow a good, intelligent person
      Who is wise, insightful, learned,
      Committed to virtue, dutiful, and noble,
As the moon follows the path of the stars.   (208)

SIXTEEN

The Dear*

Practicing what one shouldn't,
    Not practicing what one should,
Having abandoned the goal,
    Clinging to what is dear,
One comes to envy those who practice.   (209)*

Don't get entangled
    With what you long for or dislike.
Not seeing what you long for is suffering;
    So also is seeing what you dislike.   (210)*

Therefore, do not turn anything
    Into something longed for,
For then it's dreadful to lose.
    Without longing or dislike,
    No bonds exist.   (211)

Longing gives rise to grief;
      Longing gives rise to fear.
For someone released from longing
      There is no grief;
      And from where would come fear?   (212)

Affection gives rise to grief;
      Affection gives rise to fear.
For someone released from affection
      There is no grief;
      And from where would come fear?   (213)

Infatuation gives rise to grief;
      Infatuation gives rise to fear.
For someone released from infatuation
      There is no grief;
      And from where would come fear?   (214)

Sensual craving gives rise to grief;
      Sensual craving gives rise to fear.
For someone released from sensual craving
      There is no grief;
      And from where would come fear?   (215)

Craving gives rise to grief;
      Craving gives rise to fear.
For someone released from craving
      There is no grief;
      And from where would come fear?   (216)

People hold dear those
> Who have done their own work,
>> Complete in virtue and vision,
>> Established in the Dhamma,
>> And who speak the truth. (217)

Anyone who aspires to the Indescribable,
> Whose mind is expansive,
> And whose heart is not bound to sensual craving
Is called "one bound upstream." (218)*

Relatives, friends, and companions
> Rejoice
When a long-absent person
> Returns from afar.
Just so, in passing from this world to the next,
> The merit we have made
Receives us,
> As a family does the return of a beloved relative.

(219–220)

SEVENTEEN

Anger

Give up anger, give up conceit,
    Pass beyond every fetter.
There is no suffering for one who possesses nothing,
    Who doesn't cling to body-and-mind.   (221)*

The one who keeps anger in check as it arises,
    As one would a careening chariot,
I call a charioteer.
    Others are merely rein-holders.   (222)

Conquer anger with non-anger;
    Conquer wickedness with goodness;
Conquer stinginess with giving,
    And a liar with truth.   (223)

If one speaks the truth,
      Is not angry,
And gives when asked, even when one has little,
      Then one comes into the presence of the gods.

(224)

Sages who do no harm,
      Constantly restrained in body,
Go to the immovable state
      Where they do not grieve.   (225)*

For the ever-wakeful—
      Training day and night,
      Intent on Nirvana—
The toxins disappear.   (226)*

Ancient is this [saying], O Atula,
      It is not just of today:
            They find fault in one sitting silently,
            They find fault in one speaking much,
            They find fault in one speaking moderately.
            No one in this world is not found at fault.

(227)*

No person can be found
      Who has been, is, or will be
      Only criticized
      Or only praised.   (228)

Who is worthy enough to find fault
    In one who is like a coin of the finest gold—
        Blameless in conduct,
        Intelligent,
        Endowed with insight and virtue,
        Praised by the wise after being observed day
            after day?
Such a one is praised even by the gods,
    Even by Brahmā.   (229–230)*

Guard against anger erupting in your body;
    Be restrained with your body.
Letting go of bodily misconduct,
    Practice good conduct with your body.   (231)

Guard against anger erupting in your speech;
    Be restrained with your speech.
Letting go of verbal misconduct,
    Practice good conduct with your speech.   (232)

Guard against anger erupting in your mind;
    Be restrained with your mind.
Letting go of mental misconduct,
    Practice good conduct with your mind.   (233)

The wise are restrained in body,
    Restrained in speech.
The wise are restrained in mind.
    They are fully restrained.   (234)

61

EIGHTEEN

Corruption

You are now like a yellowed leaf;
    Yama's henchmen are standing by.
You stand at the door of death
    With no provisions for the journey.
Make an island for yourself.
    Be quick in making effort. Be wise.
Unblemished, with corruption removed,
    You'll enter the divine realm of the noble ones.

(235–236)*

You are now at the end of life;
    You're headed for Yama's presence
With no resting place along the way,
    No provisions for the journey.
Make an island for yourself.
    Be quick in making effort. Be wise.
Unblemished, with corruption removed,
    You'll experience birth and old age no more.

(237–238)*

As a smith does with silver,
    The wise person
Gradually,
    Bit by bit,
        Moment by moment,
Removes impurities from herself.   (239)

As rust corrupts
    The very iron that formed it,
So transgressions lead
    Their doer to states of woe.   (240)*

Oral teachings become corrupted when not recited,
    Homes are corrupted by inactivity,
Sloth corrupts [physical] beauty,
    Negligence corrupts a guardian.   (241)

Bad conduct is corruption in a person;
    Stinginess, corruption in a giver.
Evil traits corrupt people
    In both this world and the next.   (242)*

More corrupt than these
    Is ignorance, the greatest corruption.
Having abandoned this corruption,
    Monks, remain corruption-free!   (243)

Easy is life
    For someone without conscience,
    Bold as a crow,
    Obtrusive, deceitful, reckless, and corrupt.

Difficult is life
    For someone with conscience,
    Always searching for what's pure,
    Discerning, sincere, cautious, and clean-living.

(244–245)

One digs up one's own root
    Here in this very world
If one kills, lies, steals,
    Goes to another's spouse,
Or gives oneself up to drink and intoxicants.

(246–247)*

Good person, know this:
    Evil traits are reckless!
Don't let greed and wrongdoing
    Oppress you with long-term suffering.   (248)

According to their faith,
    According to their satisfaction,
People give.
    This being the case,
If one is envious
    Of the food and drink [given] to others,
One does not attain *samādhi*
    By day or by night.
But by cutting out, uprooting and discarding
    This [envious state]
One gains *samādhi*
    By day or by night.   (249–250)*

There's no fire like lust,
    No grasping like hate,
No snare like delusion,
    No river like craving.   (251)

It's easy to see the faults of others
    But hard to see one's own.
One sifts out the faults of others like chaff
    But conceals one's own,
    As a cheat conceals a bad throw of the dice.
                                              (252)

If one focuses on others' faults
    And constantly takes offense,
One's own toxins flourish
    And one is far from their destruction.   (253)

No path exists in space;
    No contemplatives exist outside [the Buddha's
        path];
People are enamored with obsessive thoughts;
    *Tathāgata*s are free of obsessive thinking.   (254)*

No path exists in space;
    No contemplatives exist outside [the Buddha's
        path];
No created things are eternal;
    No agitation exists for buddhas.   (255)*

NINETEEN

The Just*

One is not just
>	Who judges a case hastily.
A wise person considers
>	Both what is and isn't right.
Guiding others without force,
>	Impartially and in accord with the Dharma,
One is called a guardian of the Dharma,
>	Intelligent and just. (256–257)*

One is not wise
>	Only because one speaks a lot.
One who is peaceful, without hate, and fearless
>	Is said to be wise. (258)

One does not uphold the Dharma
 Only because one speaks a lot.
Having heard even a little,
 If one perceives the Dharma with one's own body
And is never negligent of the Dharma,
 Then one is indeed an upholder of the Dharma.

(259)

Gray hair does not
 Make one an elder.
Someone ripe only in years
 Is called "an old fool."
It's through truth,
 Dharma, harmlessness, restraint, and self-control
That the wise one, purged of impurities,
 Is called "an elder." (260–261)

Not through talk alone or by good looks
 Does someone envious, stingy, and treacherous
Become a person of good character.
 But with these cut off, uprooted, and destroyed,
A person wise and purged of faults
 Is called "of good character." (262–263)*

Not by means of a shaven head
    Does someone dishonest and undisciplined
Become a renunciant.
    How could someone filled with longing and greed
    Be a renunciant?
Someone who has pacified evil
    Small and great,
    In every way,
Is, for that reason, called a renunciant.   (264–265)

One is not a mendicant
    Just because one begs from others.
Nor does one become a mendicant
    By taking on domestic ways.

But whoever sets aside
    Both merit and evil,
Lives the chaste life,
    And goes through the world deliberately
Is called "a mendicant."   (266–267)*

Not by silence
    Does an ignorant fool become a sage.
The wise person, who,
    As if holding a set of scales,
Selects what's good and avoids what's evil
    Is, for that reason, a sage.
Whoever can weigh these two sides of the world
    Is, for that reason, called "a sage."   (268–269)*

Not by harming living beings
    Is one a noble one.
By being harmless to all living beings
    Is one called "a noble one."   (270)

Not with
    Virtue or religious practice,
    Great learning,
    Attaining *samādhi,*
    Dwelling alone,
    Or [thinking], "I touch the happiness
        Of renunciation unknown by ordinary
        people,"
Should you, monk, rest assured,
    Without having destroyed the toxins.   (271–272)*

TWENTY

The Path

The best of paths is the Eightfold [Path];
    The best of truths, the Four [Noble Truths].
The best of qualities is dispassion;
    And the best among gods and humans
        Is the one with eyes to see.

This is the path
    For purifying one's vision; there is no other.
Follow it,
    You'll bewilder Māra.
Follow it,
    You'll put an end to suffering.
This is the path I have proclaimed,
    Having pulled out the arrows.   (273–275)*

It is up to you to make strong effort;
    *Tathāgata*s merely tell you how.
Following the path, those absorbed in meditation
    Will be freed from Māra's bonds.   (276)*

"All created things are impermanent."
    Seeing this with insight,
One becomes disenchanted with suffering.
    This is the path to purity.   (277)*

"All created things are suffering."
    Seeing this with insight,
One becomes disenchanted with suffering.
    This is the path to purity.   (278)*

"All things are not-self."
    Seeing this with insight,
One becomes disenchanted with suffering.
    This is the path to purity.   (279)*

Inactive when one should be active,
    Lazy [though] young and strong,
Disheartened in one's resolves,
    Such an indolent, lethargic person
Doesn't find the path of insight.   (280)*

Watchful in speech and well-restrained in mind,
    Do nothing unskillful with your body.
Purify these three courses of action;
    Fulfill the path taught by the sages.   (281)

Wisdom arises from [spiritual] practice;
    Without practice it decays.
Knowing this two-way path for gain and loss,
    Conduct yourself so that wisdom grows.   (282)*

Cut down the forest [of desire], not [real] trees.
    From the forest [of desire], fear is born.
Having cut down both the forest and the underbrush,
    Monks, be deforested [of desire].   (283)*

As long as even the slightest underbrush of desire
    Between man and woman is not cut away,
For that long, the mind is bound
    Like a suckling calf is to its mother.   (284)

Destroy attachment to self
    As you could an autumn lily in your fist.
Cultivate the path to peace,
    The Nirvana taught by the Well-Gone-One.

                                                  (285)*

"Here I'll live during the rainy season,
    And here during the winter and summer."
So the fool ponders,
    Unaware of danger.
Intoxicated by children and cattle,
    That addict
Is swept away by Death,
    As a sleeping village is by a great flood.   (286–287)

Children, parents, and relatives
    Are not a protection;
For someone seized by Death,
    Relatives are no protection.
Knowing this,
    The wise person, restrained by virtue,
Should quickly clear the path
    To Nirvana.   (288–289)*

TWENTY-ONE

Miscellaneous

If, by giving up a lesser happiness,
    One could experience greater happiness,
A wise person would renounce the lesser
    To behold the greater.   (290)*

Those who seek their own happiness
    By causing suffering for others
Are entangled with hostility.
    From hostility they are not set free.   (291)

The toxins multiply
        For the insolent and negligent
Who reject what they should do
        And do instead what they should not.
But the toxins come to an end
        For those who are mindful and alert,
Who are constantly well-engaged
        With mindfulness of the body,
Who don't resort to what they should not do
        But persist in doing what they should.   (292–293)

Having killed
        Mother, father,
        Two warrior kings,
        A kingdom and its subjects,
The brahmin, undisturbed, moves on.   (294)*

Having killed
        Mother, father,
        Two learned kings,
        And a tiger,
The brahmin, undisturbed, moves on.   (295)*

Always wide awake
        Are the disciples of Gotama
Who constantly, day and night,
        Are mindful of the Buddha.   (296)

Always wide awake
      Are the disciples of Gotama
Who constantly, day and night,
      Are mindful of the Dharma.   (297)

Always wide awake
      Are the disciples of Gotama
Who constantly, day and night,
      Are mindful of the Sangha.   (298)*

Always wide awake
      Are the disciples of Gotama
Who constantly, day and night,
      Are mindful of the body.   (299)

Always wide awake
      Are the disciples of Gotama
Whose minds constantly, day and night,
      Delight in harmlessness.   (300)

Always wide awake
      Are the disciples of Gotama
Whose minds constantly, day and night,
      Delight in [spiritual] practice.   (301)*

Going forth [into homelessness] is difficult—it's hard
    to enjoy.
        Household life is difficult—it's painful.
Living with discordant people is suffering.
A traveler is subject to suffering,
        So don't be a traveler
And don't be subject to suffering.   (302)*

People endowed
        With faith, virtue, fame, and wealth
Are revered
        Wherever they go.   (303)

From afar, good people shine
        Like the Himalaya mountains.
Close up, bad people disappear
        Like arrows shot into the night.   (304)

Sitting alone, resting alone, walking alone,
        Untiring and alone,
Whoever has tamed oneself
        Will find delight in the forest.   (305)

TWENTY-TWO

Hell

Those who assert what is not true go to hell,
   As do those who deny what they've done.
Both these people of base deeds become equal
   After death, in the world beyond.   (306)

Many who wear the saffron robe
   Have evil traits and lack restraint.
By their evil deeds are these wicked people
   Reborn in hell.   (307)*

Better to eat a flaming red-hot iron ball
   Than to be an immoral and unrestrained person
Feeding on the alms-food of the people.   (308)*

Four results come to the careless person
        Who consorts with the spouse of another:
Demerit,
        Disturbed sleep,
                Disgrace,
                        And hell.
For the frightened pair
        Delight is brief
[And then comes]
        Demerit,
                Rebirth in an evil state,
                        And harsh punishment from the king.
Therefore a person should not consort with another's
        spouse.   (309–310)*

Just as *kusa* grass cuts the hand
        That wrongly grasps it,
So the renunciant life, if wrongly grasped,
        Drags one down to hell.   (311)

A lax act, corrupt practice,
        Or chaste life lived dubiously
Doesn't bear much fruit.   (312)*

With steady effort
        One should do what is to be done
Because the lax renunciant stirs up
        Even more dust.   (313)*

A foul deed is best not done—
    The foul deed torments one later.
A good deed is best done—
    For, having done it, one has no regret.   (314)

Just as a fortified city
    Is guarded inside and out,
So guard yourself—
    Don't let a moment pass you by.
Those who let the moment pass
    Grieve when they're consigned to hell.   (315)

Ashamed of what's not shameful
    And not ashamed of what is,
Those who take up wrong views
    Go to a bad rebirth.   (316)*

Seeing danger in what's not dangerous
    And not seeing danger in what is,
Those who take up wrong views
    Go to a bad rebirth.   (317)

Finding fault in what's not at fault
    And seeing no fault in what is,
Those who take up wrong views
    Go to a bad rebirth.   (318)

But knowing fault as fault,
    And the faultless as the faultless,
Those who take up right views
    Go to a good rebirth.   (319)

TWENTY-THREE

The Elephant

As an elephant in battle
    Endures an arrow shot from a bow,
So will I endure verbal abuse;
    Many people, indeed, lack virtue.   (320)

The tamed elephant is the one
    They take into a crowd.
The tamed elephant is the one
    The king mounts.
Best among humans is the tamed person
    Who endures verbal abuse.   (321)

Excellent are tamed mules,
      Thoroughbreds, horses of the Indus valley,
Tusked elephants and great elephants.
      But even more excellent
Are people who have tamed themselves.

Not by means of these animals could one go
      To that place not gone to,
Where a self-tamed person goes
      By means of a well-tamed, disciplined self.

(322–323)*

The elephant called Dhanapālaka
      Is hard to control when in rut;
Tied down, the tusker doesn't even eat,
      Remembering the elephant forest.   (324)*

The sluggish and gluttonous simpleton
      Who sleeps and rolls about
Like a fat, grain-fed hog
      Is reborn again and again.   (325)*

In the past, this mind went wandering
      Where it wished, as it liked, and as it pleased.
Now I will retrain it wisely,
      As an elephant keeper does an elephant in rut.

(326)*

Delight in vigilance.
> Protect your own mind.
Lift yourself from a bad course
> Like a tusker sunk in mud. (327)

If you find an intelligent companion,
> A fellow traveler
> A sage of good conduct,
You should travel together,
> Delighted and mindful,
> Overcoming all dangers. (328)

If you do not find an intelligent companion,
> A fellow traveler
> Of good conduct and wise,
Travel alone,
> Like a king renouncing a conquered kingdom,
> Like the elephant Matanga in the forest. (329)*

There is no companionship with a fool;
> It is better to go alone.
Travel alone, at ease, doing no evil
> Like the elephant Matanga in the forest. (330)

Happiness is having friends when need arises.

    Happiness is contentment with whatever there is.

Happiness is merit at the end of one's life.

    Happiness is the abandoning of all suffering.

In the world, respect for one's mother is happiness,

    As is respect for one's father.

In the world, respect for renunciants is happiness,

    As is respect for brahmins.

Happiness is virtue lasting through old age.

    Happiness is steadfast faith.

Happiness is the attainment of wisdom.

    Not doing evil is happiness.   (331–333)

TWENTY-FOUR

Craving

The craving of a person who lives negligently
  Spreads like a creeping vine.
Such a person leaps ever onward,
  Like a monkey seeking fruit in the forest.   (334)*

Sorrow grows
  Like grass after rain
For anyone overcome by this miserable craving
  And clinging to the world.   (335)*

Sorrow falls away
  Like drops of water from a lotus
For anyone who overcomes this miserable craving
  And clinging to the world.   (336)

This I say to you:
>Good fortune to all assembled here!
>Dig out the root of craving
>>As you would the fragrant root of *bīrana*
>>grass.
>Don't let Māra destroy you again and again,
>>As a torrential river [breaks] a reed.   (337)

Just as a felled tree grows again
>If the roots are unharmed and strong,
So suffering sprouts again and again
>Until the tendency to crave is rooted out.   (338)

With the thirty-six streams [of craving]
>Flowing mightily toward anything pleasing,
The person of wrong views
>Is carried away on the currents of lustful intent.

   (339)*

The streams flow everywhere;
>The creeper [of craving] sprouts and remains.
Seeing that the creeper has sprouted,
>Use insight to cut it at the root.   (340)

When desire flows,
>Pleasure arises.
Attached to happiness, seeking enjoyment,
>People are subject to birth and old age.   (341)

Surrounded by craving,
    People run around like frightened hares.
Held by fetters and bonds,
    They suffer, repeatedly, over a long time.   (342)

Surrounded by craving,
    People run around like frightened hares.
Seeking dispassion,
    A monastic should dispel craving.   (343)

[Though] clear of the underbrush
    And out of the forest,
Someone attached to the forest
    Runs right back to it.
Come, see that free person
    Run back into bondage.   (344)*

It's not a strong bond, say the wise,
    That is made of iron, wood, or grass.
A strong bond, say the wise,
    Is infatuation with jewels and ornaments
    And longing for children and spouse—
        That bond is weighty, elastic, and hard to
        loosen.

Having cut even this, they go forth,
      Free from longing, abandoning sensual pleasures.
Those attached to passion
      Are caught in a river [of their own making]
      Like a spider caught in its own web.
But having cut even this, the wise set forth,
      Free from longing, abandoning all suffering.

(345–347)*

Let go of the past, let go of the future,
      Let go of the present.
Gone beyond becoming,
      With the mind released in every way,
You do not again undergo birth and old age.   (348)*

For people who
      Have agitated thoughts
      And intense passion,
      And who are focused on what's pleasant,
Craving grows more and more.
      Indeed, they strengthen their bonds.

But those who
      Delight in calming their thoughts,
      Are always mindful,
      And cultivate a focus on what's unpleasant,
Will bring an end [to craving].
      They will cut Māra's bonds.   (349–350)*

Fearless, free of craving, and without blemish,
        Having reached the goal
And destroyed the arrows of becoming,
        One is in one's final body.   (351)*

Free of craving and grasping,
        Skilled in words and their usage,
Knowing the order of the teachings—
        What precedes and what follows—
One is said to be "a great person of much wisdom,
        In one's final body."   (352)*

"I am all-conquering, all-knowing,
        Stained by nothing.
Letting go of everything,
        Released through the destruction of craving
        And having known directly on my own,
Whom could I point to [as my teacher]?"   (353)*

The gift of Dharma surpasses all gifts.
        The taste of Dharma surpasses all tastes.
The delight in Dharma surpasses all delights.
        The destruction of craving conquers all suffering.

                                                       (354)

Wealth destroys those who lack in wisdom,
    But not those who seek the beyond.
Craving wealth, those lacking wisdom
    Destroy themselves
        As well as others.   (355)

Weeds are the ruin of fields;
    Passion is the ruin of people.
So offerings to those free of passion
    Bear great fruit.   (356)

Weeds are the ruin of fields;
    Ill will is the ruin of people.
So offerings to those free of ill will
    Bear great fruit.   (357)

Weeds are the ruin of fields;
    Delusion is the ruin of people.
So offerings to those free of delusion
    Bear great fruit.   (358)

Weeds are the ruin of fields;
    Longing is the ruin of people.
So offerings to those free of longing
    Bear great fruit.   (359)

TWENTY-FIVE

The Bhikkhu[*]

Restraint of the eye is good,
    Good is restraint of the ear.
Restraint of the nose is good,
    Good is restraint of the tongue.
Restraint of the body is good,
    Good is restraint of speech.
Restraint of the mind is good,
    Good is restraint in all circumstances.
Restrained in all circumstances,
    The *bhikkhu* is released from all suffering.

(360–361)*

The one with
    Hands restrained,
    Feet restrained,
    Speech restrained,

Who is foremost among the restrained,
    Inwardly delighted,
    Composed,
    Solitary,
    And contented,
Is called a *bhikkhu*.   (362)

Sweet is the speech
    Of a *bhikkhu* who
        Restrains his mouth,
        Speaks insightfully,
        Is not conceited,
        And illuminates the teaching and the goal.

                                                         (363)*

The *bhikkhu* who
    Dwells in the Dharma,
    Delights in the Dharma,
    Reflects on the Dharma,
    Recollects the Dharma,
Doesn't fall away from the true Dharma.   (364)

One shouldn't scorn what one has received,
    Nor envy others.
The mendicant who envies others
    Doesn't become concentrated.   (365)*

The gods praise the mendicant
Who lives purely and untiringly
And who doesn't scorn
What he or she receives,
Even if receiving just a little.   (366)

Anyone who doesn't cherish as "mine"
Anything of body-and-mind
And who doesn't grieve for that which doesn't exist,
Is indeed called a *bhikkhu*.   (367)*

A *bhikkhu* dwelling in loving-kindness
And pleased with the Buddha's teachings
Attains happiness, the stilling of formations,
The state of peace.   (368)

Bhikkhu, bail out this boat.
Emptied, it will move quickly for you.
Cutting off passion and aversion,
You will go to Nirvana.   (369)

Cut off the five [lower fetters];
Let go of the five [higher fetters];
Above all, cultivate the five [faculties].
A *bhikkhu* who surmounts five attachments
Is called "someone who has crossed the flood."   (370)*

Bhikkhu, be absorbed in meditation;
     Don't be negligent;
Don't let your mind whirl about
     In sensual desire.
Don't be negligent and swallow a [molten] iron ball,
     And then, being burnt, cry out,
"This is suffering!"   (371)

There is no meditative absorption
     For one without insight.
There is no insight
     For one without meditative absorption.
With both,
     One is close to Nirvana.   (372)*

For a *bhikkhu* with a peaceful mind,
     Who enters an empty dwelling
And clearly sees the true Dharma,
     There is superhuman joy.   (373)*

Fully knowing
     The arising and passing of the *khandha*s,
One attains joy and delight.
     For those who know, this is the Deathless.

                                 (374)*

The starting point for an insightful *bhikkhu* is
    Guarding the senses,
    Contentment,
    Restraint according to the monastic rules,
    And associating with good spiritual friends
        Who live purely and untiringly.   (375)

If one is friendly by habit
    And skillful in conduct,
One will have much delight
    And bring an end to suffering.   (376)

As jasmine sheds its withered flowers
    So, *bhikkhu*s, shed passion and aversion.   (377)

Peaceful in body, peaceful in speech,
    The *bhikkhu* peaceful and well-concentrated
Who has rejected the world's bait
    Is called "one at peace."   (378)*

Admonish yourself.
    Control yourself.
O *bhikkhu,* self-guarded and mindful,
    You will live happily.   (379)

Oneself, indeed, is one's own protector.
   One does, indeed, [make] one's own destiny.
Therefore, control yourself
   As a merchant does a fine horse.   (380)

A *bhikkhu* filled with delight
   And pleased with the Buddha's teachings
Attains happiness, the stilling of formations,
   The state of peace.   (381)

Engaged in the Buddha's teachings,
   Even a young *bhikkhu*
Lights up this world
   Like the moon
   Set free from a cloud.   (382)

TWENTY-SIX

The Brahmin[*]

Strive and cut off the stream.
    O brahmin, dispel sensual craving.
Knowing the ending of all formations,
    You, brahmin, will know the Unmade.   (383)

When, with tranquillity and insight,
    The brahmin reaches the other shore,
Then for that "knowing one"
    All fetters come to their end.   (384)*

Whoever is
    Untied and free of distress,
And for whom neither a "beyond," a "not-beyond,"
    Nor a "both beyond-and-not-beyond" exist,
I call a brahmin.   (385)*

Whoever is
> Seated, absorbed in meditation,
> Done what had to be done,
> Free of contaminants,
> Who has reached the highest goal,

I call a brahmin.   (386)

The sun shines by day.
> The moon glows at night.

The warrior shines in his armor.
> The brahmin shines in meditative absorption.

But all day and all night,
> The Buddha shines in splendor.   (387)

Having banished evil,
> One is called a brahmin.

Living peacefully,
> One is called a renunciant.

Having driven out one's own impurities,
> One is called "one who has gone forth."   (388)*

One should not strike a brahmin
> And a brahmin should not set [anger] loose.

Shame on the one who hits a brahmin
> And greater shame on the one who sets [anger]
> loose.   (389)*

For the brahmin, nothing is better
        Than restraining the mind
        From what it cherishes.
Whenever one turns away from the intent to harm,
        Suffering is allayed.   (390)

Whoever does no ill
        Through body, speech, and mind,
And is restrained in these three areas,
        I call a brahmin.   (391)

As a brahmin worships a ritual fire,
        One should respectfully worship
Anyone from whom one might learn
        The Dharma of the Fully Self-Awakened One.

                                                 (392)*

Not by matted hair, not by clan,
        Not by birth does one become a brahmin.
The one in whom there is truth and Dharma
        Is the one who is pure, is a brahmin.   (393)

Fool! What use is matted hair?
        What use is a deerskin robe?
The tangled jungle is within you
        And you groom the outside!   (394)

Someone robed in discarded rags,
    Lean, with veins showing,
Alone in the forest, absorbed in meditation,
    I call a brahmin.   (395)

I call no one a brahmin
    For being born from a womb, from a mother.
Someone who has anything
    Is called "self-important."
Whoever has nothing and does not cling,
    I call a brahmin.   (396)*

Whoever, having cut off every fetter,
    Does not tremble,
Is unbound and beyond attachment,
    I call a brahmin.   (397)*

Whoever, awakened, has cut
    The strap, thong, cord, and bridle,
And lifted up the crossbar,
    I call a brahmin.   (398)*

Whoever endures abuse, assault, and imprisonment
    Without animosity,
And who has forbearance as one's strength,
    As one's mighty army,
I call a brahmin.   (399)

Whoever is without anger or craving,
        Observant in spiritual practice and virtue,
Self-controlled, and in one's final body,
        I call a brahmin.   (400)*

Like water on a lotus leaf,
        Or a mustard seed on the tip of an awl,
Whoever does not cling to sensual craving,
        I call a brahmin.   (401)

Whoever knows, right here,
        The ending of suffering,
Who is unburdened and unbound,
        I call a brahmin.   (402)

Whoever is wise,
        Of profound insight,
Understanding what is and isn't the path,
        And who has attained the highest goal,
I call a brahmin.   (403)

Whoever is not mixed up with
        Householders or renunciants,
Who has no abode and few desires,
        I call a brahmin.   (404)*

Having given up violence
Toward beings both timid and strong,
Whoever neither kills nor causes others to kill,
I call a brahmin.   (405)*

Whoever is unopposing among those who oppose,
Peaceful among the violent,
Not clinging among those who cling,
I call a brahmin.   (406)*

Whoever lets passion, aversion,
Conceit, and hypocrisy fall away
Like a mustard seed from the tip of an awl,
I call a brahmin.   (407)

Whoever speaks
What is true, informative, and not harsh,
Who gives offense to no one,
I call a brahmin.   (408)

Whoever in this world
Takes nothing not given,
Whether it is long or short,
Large or small,
Beautiful or not,
I call a brahmin.   (409)

Whoever has no longing
    For this world or the beyond,
Who is unbound and without longing,
    I call a brahmin.   (410)

Having no attachments,
    And, through understanding, free of doubts,
Whoever is established in the Deathless
    I call a brahmin.   (411)*

Whoever here has overcome attachments
    For both merit and evil
And who is sorrowless, dustless, and pure,
    I call a brahmin.   (412)

Whoever, like the moon,
    Is spotless, pure, clear, and undisturbed,
In whom the delight for existence is extinct,
    I call a brahmin.   (413)*

Whoever has passed beyond this troublesome road,
    This difficult path, this samsara, this delusion,
Who has crossed over, gone beyond,
    Who is a meditator, free of craving and doubt,
Without clinging, released,
    I call a brahmin.   (414)*

Whoever, having given up passion here,
    Would go forth as a "homeless one,"
In whom the passion for existence is extinct,
    I call a brahmin. (415)*

Whoever, having given up craving here,
    Would go forth as a "homeless one,"
In whom the craving for existence is extinct,
    I call a brahmin. (416)*

Whoever, having given up human bondage,
    Has gone beyond heavenly bondage,
Is unbound from all bondage,
    I call a brahmin. (417)

Whoever, having given up liking and disliking,
    Has become cooled, without attachments,
A hero overcoming the entire world,
    I call a brahmin. (418)*

Whoever knows in every way
    The passing away and reappearing of beings,
And is unattached, awakened, and well-gone,
    I call a brahmin. (419)*

An arahant, whose destination is not known
      By gods, *gandhabba*s, or humans,
Whose toxins are extinct,
      I call a brahmin.   (420)*

One for whom nothing exists
      In front, behind, and in between,
Who has no clinging, who has nothing,
      I call a brahmin.   (421)*

Whoever is most excellent, a bull,
      A hero, a great sage, a conqueror,
Free of craving, cleansed, awakened,
      I call a brahmin.   (422)

Whoever
      Knows [one's own] former lives,
      Sees both the heavens and states of woe,
      Has attained the end of birth,
      Is a sage, perfected in the higher knowledges,
      And has perfected all perfections,
I call a brahmin.   (423)

Afterword

ABOUT THE TEXT

THE *Dhammapada* IS ONE OF THE TEXTS THAT HAVE come to comprise the canon of Theravada Buddhism. This extensive body of scriptures is organized into three major collections (*tipiṭaka,* literally "three baskets"): the Vinaya Piṭaka ("basket of discipline"), which is concerned with monastic discipline and regulations; the Sutta Piṭaka ("basket of teachings"), which records teachings and discussions by the Buddha and some of his chief disciples; and the Abhidhamma Piṭaka ("basket of special teaching"), which consists of detailed philosophical and psychological analyses of the teachings found in the Sutta Piṭaka. The Sutta Piṭaka is itself divided into five collections of texts, or *nikāya*s. The *Dhammapada* is one of fifteen texts belonging to the collection known as the *Khuddaka Nikāya,* or "Section of Short Sayings."

In addition to holding a place within the Theravada canon, the *Dhammapada* belongs to a family of closely related texts that have been called the Dharmapada genre of literature (using the Sanskrit word), with the *Dhammapada* being the only representative of this genre preserved in Pali. Other members of this family belonging to the canons of Buddhist traditions other than the Theravada have survived in Gāndharī, Sanskrit, Tibetan, and Chinese. All are anthologies of verses, although they do not use all the same verses or the same ordering of verses and chapters. Some of the anthologies have considerably more verses than does the Pali *Dhammapada*. The bibliography provides references for some of the extant works of this family of texts.

From the existence of the various Dharmapada texts we can conclude that ancient Indian Buddhist editors made many such verse anthologies, the contents of which were fluid. The process of selecting, excluding, and arranging the verses continued over an extended period of time within diverse Buddhist communities. It is not possible to discern which anthology is of greatest antiquity or which may have served as a basis for others. Scholars of the Dharmapada literature generally believe that the process of compiling Dharmapada texts began well before any of the surviving versions were finalized, and that there was a complex interplay of influence among the different anthologies that were

being composed. It may well be that the work of selecting and arranging verses began during or soon after
the time of the Buddha. The surviving records do not
reveal when any of the existing Dharmapada texts, including the Pali version, attained their present form.

Later Theravada commentaries take for granted
that the *Dhammapada* is a collection of verses spoken
by the Buddha and recount stories, mostly apocryphal,
of the occasion on which the Buddha spoke each verse.
Only 166 of the verses have parallels elsewhere in the
Sutta Piṭaka and the Vinaya Piṭaka (see the appendix
on page 147). Though most of these 166 parallel verses
are presented as the words of the Buddha, more than
30 are presented as spoken by one of his disciples or by
a god. One might argue that these speakers are simply
repeating verses the Buddha spoke on another occasion. However, in the sutta passage containing the parallel to verse 383, the Buddha praises a god for this
verse and encourages people to memorize it, which
suggests that the Buddha did not consider the verse to
be his own (*Saṃyutta Nikāya* 1.49–50). In another
passage, the Buddha explains that lines now found in
verse 204 of the *Dhammapada* did not originate with
himself but were already current in the society of his
day (*Majjhima Nikāya* 75.19–21). Furthermore, a
number of verses appear independently in non-Buddhist Indian sources, suggesting they were selected
from a wider body of poems circulating in ancient

India. Although the great majority of verses may have originated with the Buddha, the evidence argues against the claim that they have all so originated. But as a body of verses selected and organized by followers of the Buddha, the *Dhammapada* is valuable in part because it helps us to understand how ancient Indian Buddhists presented their understanding of how to be Buddhists.

Some scholars have tried to discern logic in the arrangement of verses and chapters of the *Dhammapada*. Most common is the suggestion that the opening two verses appear at the start of the text because they emphasize the basic principle of the central role of one's own mind and behavior, which is the basis for all the other verses. A more obvious logic is that most of the verses in each chapter (except for chapter 21, "Miscellaneous") are linked to a particular concept or word that is represented by the chapter title. However, verses in a chapter may have little in common with one another except for a (sometimes minimal) connection to the chapter title. As discussed in the introduction, some chapters seem to be paired to present the two sides of a dichotomy, e.g., the wise and the fool, Buddha and the world, craving and the monk who overcomes craving. Aside from this, there is little to indicate what, if any, significance is to be found in the arrangement of verses and chapters. In various Sanskrit and Chinese versions of the Dharmapada texts, the chapters and verses appear in very different orders. For example, the first two verses of the *Dhammapada* do not appear until the middle of the thirty-first chapter of the *Udānavarga*, one of the Sanskrit Dharmapada texts.

Yet the lack of a coherent logic or order does not necessarily mean that the Pali text is a random collection of dissociated pieces. Its development over time suggests that various editors have worked with the text to try to express their understandings of the Buddha's path. To the degree that the *Dhammapada* is a consciously selected anthology of verses, it is important to take the text as a whole. Removing any part of the *Dhammapada*, selecting the stanzas one finds inspiring and removing or rewriting the difficult or uninteresting ones, would leave a skewed picture of how ancient Buddhists understood their lives and spiritual practice.

Down through the centuries Buddhism has been transmitted from person to person, from warm hand to warm hand. No matter how much Buddhism has evolved and changed over time, it remains a descendant of the ancient Indian Buddhists who laid the foundation for the tradition. I have translated the *Dhammapada* with the idea that it is valuable to try to understand these ancestors.

Notes

NUMBERS REFER TO VERSE NUMBER. DHPA REFERS TO THE *Dhammapadaṭṭhakathā*, the standard, traditional Theravada commentary on the *Dhammapada*.

Pali translations in parentheses follow the English chapter titles below.

CHAPTER 1. DICHOTOMIES (YAMAKA)

Yamaka is usually translated as "pairs" or "twins." I have chosen "dichotomies" to highlight the fact that the paired concepts in this chapter and through much of the *Dhammapada* are opposites, e.g., good and evil, wise and foolish.

1–2. The opening lines of both verses are among the more difficult lines in the *Dhammapada* to translate into English because of the ambiguity of *dhamma* (here rendered as "experience") and *mano* ("mind"). In the traditional Buddhist list of the six senses and their respective objects (*āyatana*), *mano* refers to the sixth sense, cognitive consciousness, and *dhamma* refers to what is cognized, that is, anything within the sphere of empirical experience. *Dhamma* can also refer more specifically to mental states, as the word has been rendered in some other English translations of these verses.

The expression "made by mind" translates *manomaya*. Among the family of Dharmapada anthologies, the Pali *Dhammapada* is unique in using this expression. All the other anthologies use "impelled by the mind" (*manojavā* in the Patna *Dharmapada*). Even the Chinese *Fa Jyu Jing*, the *Dharmapada* most closely related to the Pali text, gives a word meaning "mind-impelled."

5. *Vera,* here translated as "hatred,"can also be rendered "enmity" or "hostility." It is less clear how to translate *avera*, because in Pali the negative prefix *a-* can refer either to the absence of what is being negated or to its opposite. In the few occurrences of *avera* elsewhere in the Pali discourses of the Buddha, the term refers simply to the absence of hate. DhpA explains that *avera* refers to the absence of hate, as well as the presence of patience and loving-kindness. To translate *avera* as "love" probably does not do justice to the original. (See Ivo Fiser, "Pāli averam, Dhammapada 5," in A. K. Narain, ed., *Studies in Pali and Buddhism: A Memorial Volume in Honor of Bhikkhu Jagdish Kasyap* (New Delhi: B.R. Publishing, 1979), pp. 93–97.) "Truth" in the final line is a translation of *dhammo*.

6. It is unclear what *yamāmase* means, here translated as "we here must die." It may be derived from the root *yam*, "to restrain." In this case the first two lines might read "Others do not realize that we should be restrained." Or, if read *yama-amase*, it may stem from Yama, the name of the ruler of the kingdom of death, in which case it could mean "going into the presence of Yama (Death)." The commentary allows for both meanings (DhpA 1.65–66).

7–8. "Focused on the pleasant" is a translation of *subhānupassiṃ*. To focus on or contemplate the unpleasant (*asubhānupassiṃ*) is a classic mindfulness exercise used to overcome lust and attachment to the body.

9–10. These verses contain a word play between *kāsāva* (the yellow or ocher robe of a Buddhist monastic) and *kasāva* (meaning either "defilements" or a reddish yellow color). "Purged" in verse 10 is a translation of *vanta*, literally "vomited."

11–12. *Sāra*, here translated as "essential," also refers to that which is most excellent.

13–14. "Lust" is a translation of *rāga*, often translated as "passion."

17–18. *Duggatiṃ gato* ("reborn in realms of woe") literally means "gone to a bad destination." *Sugatiṃ gato* ("reborn in realms of bliss," i.e., the heavenly realms) literally is "gone to a good destination (*sugatiṃ*)." *Gati* ("destination, course") refers to one's destination after death.

CHAPTER 2. VIGILANCE (APPAMĀDA)

Appamāda could also be translated as "diligence, heedfulness, watchfulness." It is often taken to be a form of energetic mindfulness. DhpA explains that it is a synonym for constant mindfulness. It could perhaps be translated as "attentiveness."

21. "The Deathless" (*amata*), a favorite synonym for the state of liberation, is a very important and powerful word in the early

Buddhist tradition. The person who attains final liberation is freed from the cycles of rebirth. If one is not reborn, the dying that inevitably follows birth will not occur, and so it can be said that the person has attained the deathless state. In the *Dhammapada,* the term "Deathless" stands in contrast to the frequent references to Māra, the one who brings death.

22. The "noble ones" are those who have attained any one of the four traditional stages of Liberation, or Awakening: stream entry, once-returning, non-returning, and arahantship. People attaining any of the stages have the experience of Nirvana in common. The stages are distinguished by the degree to which the experience of Nirvana frees a person from the fetters that bind one to the cycles of rebirth. An arahant (a person who is fully awakened) is liberated from all the fetters and so will not be reborn again. A non-returner is freed from enough attachments that he or she will not return to a human birth; rather he or she will be reborn in a heavenly realm in which to complete the process of liberation. A once-returner retains enough attachments to be reborn as a human one last time before attaining final liberation. While the stream-enterer retains the most attachments, that person is said to have entered the stream of the Dharma that will inevitably lead to final liberation within seven lifetimes at the most.

23. "Absorbed in meditation" is a translation of *jhāyino.* Some translators understand the term to be limited to the practice of *jhāna* (meditative absorption). While this may be the case here, I understand the term to also mean meditation in general. My translation attempts to accommodate both meanings.

"Rest from toil" is a translation of *yogakkhema. Yoga* here means either bonds/attachments or undertaking/effort (see, e.g.,

Dīgha Nikāya 3.230). *Khema* can mean "peace, calm, safety, security." An alternative translation could be "safety from bondage." I choose "rest from toil" to highlight the strong contrast between the effort of practice described earlier in the verse and the goal of that effort.

25. "Flood" symbolizes the flood of ignorance and craving that overwhelms humanity. Various lists of "floods" are given in the discourses of the Buddha found in the Pali canon, the most common being attachment to sensuality, becoming, views, and ignorance (*Dhīgha Nikāya* 3.230).

30. The text uses the somewhat unusual epithet Maghavan (literally, "the Munificent") to refer to Indra, the king of the gods.

CHAPTER 3. THE MIND (CITTA)

37. *Ekacaraṁ*, here translated as "solitary," literally means "walking or roaming alone." Using later Buddhist theories of mind, the DhpA commentary explains that consciousness occurs singularly, meaning no two conscious states occur simultaneously. Another possible explanation for the solitary nature of the mind is that a person's consciousness does not directly touch or interact with someone else's consciousness.

Guhāsayaṁ, (literally "lying in a cave") is translated here as "hidden." In addition to meaning "a cave," *guhā* can refer to any hiding place. The DhpA explains that the cave refers to the heart as the seat of consciousness and to the body made up of the four physical elements (earth, water, heat, and wind).

39. *Anavassutacittassa* is traditionally understood to be a mind not overflowing, oozing, or soaked with lust. *Ananvāhacetaso* is taken to refer to a heart or to thoughts not afflicted by hate.

40. *Anivesano* ("clinging to nothing") could also be rendered "without settling [for what has been gained]."

42. *Pāpa* is here translated as "harm."

Chapter 4. Flowers (puppha)

44, 45. Yama is the ruler of the unfortunate realms of birth, such as the realms of hell, hungry ghosts, the jealous demon-gods, and animals. Sometimes he is understood to be the same as Māra. "Dharma teaching" translates *dhammapada*. See preface for a discussion of this word and other possible English translations. "One in training" (*sekho*) refers to someone still training to become an arahant, or fully awakened person.

47. DhpA compares flowers in this verse to the objects of sense desire.

48. *Antako,* here rendered as "Death," literally means "the end-maker" and is a synonym for both Māra and death.

54. "Virtuous person" (*sappuriso*).

59. "Common people" (*puthujjane*). The "Fully Awakened One" refers to the Buddha.

Chapter 5. The Fool (bāla)

Bāla originally meant a young child who is not yet able to speak. It is therefore sometimes translated as "the childish."

70. Bāla (fool) is here translated as "foolish ascetic" for purposes of clarity. In the original text, the grass is referred to as *kusa* grass; its Latin name is given in the *Pāli Text Society Dictionary* as *Poa cynosuroides*. Monier-Williams says it is a sacred grass with long pointed stalks, used in certain ceremonies.

71. "Curdle" is a translation of *muccati*. It is not obvious whether this verb should be read as a variant spelling of *mucchati* ("congeal, curdle") or as the passive present of *muñcati* ("release, emit"). The Pali commentarial tradition reads it as "curdle," whereas most non-Pali Dharmapada texts have it as "release." In the Sarvāstivāda *Abhidharma-mahāvibhāṣa-śāstra* this verse appears with this verb meaning "curdle." Here I go along with the commentarial interpretation of this verb. If the verb were to be translated as "release," the line could read "Evil deeds done are not like fresh milk that comes out quickly." In other words, the karmic products of evil deeds do not appear immediately.

72. *Ñattaṃ*, translated here as "reasoning," refers to one's intellectual faculty. The DhpA commentary (ii.73) explains that it means understanding, knowledge, intelligence, learning, or skill. The commentary also says that it refers to the fame the fool attains based on his or her ability.

75. *Viveka* ("solitude") is sometimes translated as "seclusion" or "detachment."

CHAPTER 6. THE SAGE (PAṆḌITA)

79. "Drinks in the Dharma" is a translation of *dhammapīti*. Since *pīti* can also mean "delight," the phrase could also be

rendered "delights in the Dharma." Perhaps both meanings were originally intended. "Noble ones" is a rendering of the word *ariya,* which is the most common title for those people who have attained one of the four stages of liberation.

83. "Let go" is a translation of *cajanti.* Instead of *cajanti,* a number of the editions of the Pali *Dhammapada* have *vajanti,* "go," in which case the first line could be translated "Virtuous people go everywhere."

84. "Truth" translates *dhamma.* Because *dhamma* has a broader meaning than just "truth," perhaps the term should be left untranslated.

87. *Dhamma,* here translated as "ways," could, in this verse, also mean "activities," "qualities or states of being," or "teachings." "Dark" is anything that is unskillful, evil, or deadening.

88. "Having nothing" translates *akiñcano.* It is uncertain what this term means. *Kiñcana* literally means "something" or "anything." Since a few of the early Buddhist discourses (e.g., DN 3.217) define *kiñcana* as "lust, hatred, delusion," *akiñcano* could also mean something like "without defilements."

89. The Factors of Awakening are mindfulness, investigation of dharmas, effort, joy, tranquillity, concentration, and equanimity. The personal cultivation of these factors was considered important in the spiritual practice taught by the Buddha. "Toxins" translates *āsava,* which is sometimes rendered into English as "effluents," "intoxicants," or "cankers." It seems that the word originally meant both the intoxicating juice of a plant and the discharge from a sore. In the psychological meaning used in

Buddhist texts, it usually refers to the craving for sensuality, becoming or existence, views, and ignorance. "Having destroyed the *āsava*s" is the most common description of an arahant, a fully liberated person.

CHAPTER 7. THE ARAHANT (ARAHANTA)

90. *Gataddhino,* here rendered "someone at the journey's end," refers to someone who has completed the journey or course of Buddhist practice.

92–93. "The freedom of emptiness and signlessness" is a translation of *suññato animitto ca vimokkho.* Here, emptiness and signlessness are attributes of Nirvana; in other words, Nirvana is empty of self and of greed, hate, and delusion, and it has no attributes or signs that awareness can focus on.

95. *Subbato,* translated here as "well-practiced," derives from the prefix *su* meaning "good, well," and *vata,* meaning a religious practice, rite, observance, duty, or vow. The commentaries explain that the phrase "a pillar of Indra" refers to the main column that stood at the entrance to a city, with half its length buried underground. The pillar is thus a metaphor for firmness; it is also taken as a metaphor for imperturbability, because the pillar was indifferent to either worship or disrespect given to it. Here I have translated *saṃsāra* (literally, "faring on") as "wandering." *Saṃsāra* refers to the process of transmigration, i.e., being reborn in repeated cycles of birth and death. A more literal translation of this line would be "[For such a one] saṃsāra does not arise/occur."

97. "Unmade" (*akata*) is a synonym for Nirvana. "Severed the link" (*sandicchedo*) refers to the link between death and re-

birth. This verse is filled with puns and is sometimes taken as a riddle. In addition to having literal value as translated here, it may have also been composed for shock value, as it could alternatively be translated:

> The person who is without faith and gratitude,
>> Who breaks into homes,
> Who has destroyed opportunities,
>> And who has vomited,
> Is an audacious person. [Or perhaps: Is the ultimate servant.]

CHAPTER 8. THOUSANDS (SAHASSA)

102. *Dhammapada* is here translated as "a line of Dharma."

105. A *gandhabba* is a heavenly musician. *Brahmā* is the chief of the gods in the early Buddhist pantheon.

110–111. *Asamāhito,* here rendered as "unsettled," also may mean "unconcentrated," "uncomposed," or "uncentered."

113. "The arising and passing of things," a translation of *udayavyayaṃ,* refers to one of the important insights leading to wisdom and liberation. The ancient commentary interprets it to mean the arising and passing of the five component aspects (*khandha*s) of the human being that are commonly clung to as some form of self-identity. When their transitory nature is seen, the clinging tends to be released. The five *khandha*s are form, feelings, perceptions, formations, and consciousness.

114. "Deathless" translates *amataṃ padaṃ* (literally, "the Deathless state" or "the path to the Deathless").

Chapter 9. Evil (pāpa)

119. In the last line, *pāpa* is translated as "misfortune" rather than "evil."

124. The last line could more literally be translated "Evil doesn't exist for someone not doing it." The word *pāpa* ("evil") refers both to the cause and the result, that is, both the bad deed and the unfortunate karmic results.

Chapter 10. Violence (daṇḍa)

Daṇḍa literally refers to a stick or rod that might be used for administering punishment or for fighting. I have taken the term to represent violence in general, though in verse 135 I have translated it as "stick."

129–130. *Attānaṃ upamaṃ katvā,* here translated as "seeing others as being like yourself," literally means "having made oneself the example/comparison."

142. *Niyata,* which I have translated here as "assured," is usually understood as the certainty that comes with the attainment of one of the four stages of liberation. (See endnote to v. 22, p. 118.) As such it also refers to the certainty of final release from *saṃsāra.* "Peace" translates *sama,* which could also be translated as "harmony."

143. In the *Saṃyutta Nikāya* (1.18), this verse is followed by the following verse that answers the question asked in the first.

> Few are those restrained by conscience,
>   Who are always mindful;

Few, having brought suffering to an end,
    Are in harmony among those who are not.

144. *Saṃvega* ("alarmed") describes a deep religious stirring or agitation of the heart in the face of the magnitude of the world's suffering.

Chapter 11. Old Age (jarā)

147. "Beautified body" is a translation of *cittakata* (adorned, dressed up, painted) and *bimba* (shape, image).

148. "Body" (*rūpa*).

151. The meaning of the last two lines is unclear. I interpret them to mean that the Dharma does not decay because it is renewed in the lives of good, virtuous people.

153–154. According to the commentarial tradition, these two verses were the first words the Buddha spoke after his Awakening. The commentaries explain that "house" refers to individuality, selfhood, or the body. The builder is one's craving. The rafters are the defilements. The ridgepole is ignorance. Interestingly, there is no canonical evidence that the Buddha spoke this verse. The verse does appear in the *Theragāthā*, a collection of verses spoken by the liberated disciples of the Buddha. There the verse is attributed to a monk named Sivaka (*Theragāthā* 183–184).

155. In the Buddhist discourses, gaining wealth through ethical means was considered an appropriate goal for the laity.

NOTES

CHAPTER 12. ONESELF (ATTA)

157. "In any part of the night" could more literally be translated, "During one [or: any] of the three watches of the night."

164. The *kaṭṭhaka* reed may be a kind of bamboo.

CHAPTER 13. THE WORLD (LOKA)

167. "Engrossed" is a rendering of *vaddhano*. DhpA does not explain this word, and modern translators express uncertainty as to how to translate it. It seems to mean something along the lines of both increasing and being attached. *Lokavaddhano* has been translated variably as "busy with the world" (Thanissaro), "a world-augmenter" (Carter), "worldly" (Norman), "world-upholder" (Nārada), and "linger in worldly existence" (Buddharakkhita).

173. *Kusala* ("wholesome") is more literally translated as "skillful."

175. "Psychic powers" (*iddhi*).

176. "In this one way" is a translation of *ekaṃ dhammaṃ*. Where this same verse appears in *Itivuttaka* 25, *ekaṃ dhammaṃ* clearly refers to the principle of truthfulness.

178. "Stream entry" refers to the attainment of the first of the four stages of Awakening, or enlightenment. (See note to v. 22, p. 118.)

CHAPTER 14. THE BUDDHA (BUDDHA)

In the early Buddhist literature, *Buddha* is an epithet mostly used to refer to Gotama Sakkamuni (Sanskrit: Gautama Shakyamuni), the historical Buddha. Occasionally the early literature uses it to refer to fully enlightened disciples of the Buddha and to previous buddhas who lived eons ago. As an epithet the word can be translated as "the Awakened One."

184. "Contemplative" is used to translate *samana* (spiritual renunciant).

190–192. For many Buddhists these three verses refer to the central elements of their faith. The Triple Refuge of Buddha, Dharma, and Sangha is the main focus of inspiration and reverence. The Four Noble Truths are the essential orientation or framework used to find and engage in the path to liberation. The Eightfold Path (the fourth of the Four Noble Truths) describes the practices that make up the path to be walked, namely, Right View, Right Intention, Right Speech, Right Acton, Right Livelihood, Right Effort, Right Mindfulness, and Right Concentration.

194. *Tapas,* here translated as "ardent practice," in this context could perhaps simply be translated as "practice."

195–196. "Obsessive thinking" is a translation of *papañca.* This is a difficult term to translate. Some other translations have been: proliferation, elaboration, exaggeration, complications, preoccupying tendencies, and diversified world.

CHAPTER 15. HAPPINESS (SUKHA)

197. "Ah" is used to translate the particle *vata,* an utterance of strong emotional expression or exclamation. It is sometimes translated as "surely," "indeed," "alas," or "I say!"

199. *Ussuka,* here translated as "ambition," is defined by the *Pāli Text Society Dictionary* as "endeavoring, eager." Other translations have been: busyness, restlessness, striving, full of care. Its negative, *anussuka,* means "free from greed."

200. Radiant Gods (*ābhassarā*) are a class of gods (*devā*) found in the Brahma heavens whose existence is characterized by the boundless joy of loving-kindness.

202. "Aggregates" (*khandha;* Sanskrit: *skandha*) refers to the five categories of psycho-physical phenomena from which one's sense of self is created: form, feeling, perceptions, mental formations, and consciousness.

203. *Saṅkhāra*s refers either to all compounded, fabricated things or, more specifically, to the mental world of dispositions, intentions, memories, and thought. It is often translated into English as "formations." In verses 277 and 278 I have translated it as "created things," and in verse 368 as "formations."

CHAPTER 16. THE DEAR (PIYA)

Piya is a difficult word to translate, and I have rendered it differently in different verses. As an adjective it is used to describe something or someone as dear, beloved, liked, agreeable, or pleasing. The verbal root pṛ, from which it derives, means "to hold dear, to like, to be fond of." In verse 157 I have translated *piya* as "precious."

209. Some form of the word *yoga* appears five times in this verse. *Yoga* has a range of meanings but here could mean exertion, striving, application, spiritual practice, or task. I have translated it as "practice" with the idea that it refers to Buddhist spiritual practice. "Goal" translates *attham,* a word that can also mean "purpose, aim, meaning, gain, welfare, benefit."

210. "What you long for" (*piya*); "what you dislike" (*apiya*).

218. "Indescribable" is a translation of *anakkhāte* and is synonymous with Nirvana. The commentaries explain that a person who is "bound upstream" refers to someone who has attained the third stage of Awakening and is thus a non-returner (see note for verse 22). Such a person will be reborn "upstream" in the stream of life and death into one of the more elevated heavenly realms and from there attain the final stage of Awakening.

CHAPTER 17. ANGER (KODHA)

221. "Possesses nothing" (*akiñcana;* see note to verse 88). *Nā-marūpa,* here translated as "body-and-mind," is usually translated as "name and form" and refers to all that we experience as our psycho-physical self.

225. "Immovable state" (*accutaṃ ṭhānaṃ*) is understood in the Theravada tradition as referring to Nirvana. Other translation

choices have included "unshakable abode" and "unwavering state."

226. Toxins (*āsavā*). See note to verse 89.

227. The commentarial tradition names Atula as a lay follower of the Buddha. The tradition preserves a story that the Buddha spoke this verse to Atula after he was critical of discourses given by a number of the Buddha's senior disciples.

230. Brahmā is the god who rules over the heavenly realms above the sensual-realm heavens.

CHAPTER 18. CORRUPTION (MALA)

235. Yama is the god of the underworld. (See note to verses 44–45, p. 120.) "Door of death" (*uyyogamukhe*; literally, "door of departure").

238. *Dīpa*, here translated as "island," also means "lamp" and could be so translated. I give "island" because it seems in keeping with the image of floods used elsewhere in the *Dhammapada*, e.g., verses 25 and 47. It is also how the traditional commentary understands it.

240. "States of woe" translates *duggatiṃ* ("bad destination or course") and refers to rebirth in the lower realms of existence, i.e., in the realms of animals, hungry ghosts, and hell. The entire verse is more literally translated thus:

> As rusts springs from iron
> And then corrodes that from which it has sprung,

> So the deeds of one who transgresses
> Lead one toward a bad destination.

242. *Itthiyā*, here rendered as "person," literally means "a woman." "Evil traits" translates *pāpakā dhammā*.

246. "Goes to another's spouse" translates *paradāraṃ ca gacchati*, which more literally means "goes with another's wife." It is possible that *dāraṃ* here refers to any woman who is under the protection of a man (e.g., a daughter living with her father).

249. "Envious" translates *maṅku*, which is usually taken to mean "troubled, confused, discontented." The verse seems to be referring to monastics who eat only the alms-food that the laity offer every day. Being troubled by comparing one's own alms with what other monastics had received was probably a real issue in the early Buddhist monastic community. *Samādhi* refers to a state of intense concentration. It is usually associated with meditation.

254. *Padaṃ*, here translated "path," could also be translated as "footprints." "Contemplative" is a translation of *samaṇo*, elsewhere translated as "renunciant." "Obsessive thoughts" translates *papañcā* (discussed in note to verses 195–196).

255. "Created things" translates *saṅkhārā*. (See note to verse 203.)

CHAPTER 19. THE JUST (DHAMMAṬṬHA)

The Pali word *dhammaṭṭha* could also be translated as "established in the Dharma," "firm in the Dharma," or simply "righteous."

256. *Sahasā*, here translated as "hastily," also can mean "inconsiderately."

262–263. "Of good character" (*sādhurūpa*).

266–267. "Domestic ways" is a translation of *vissaṃ dhammaṃ*. It is unclear how to understand *vissaṃ*; we find a wide range of English translations. I have gone along with both John Ross Carter's and K. R. Norman's suggestions that it is derived from *visma*, meaning "house" or "domestic." The *Dhammapada* commentary (3.393) suggests that it means either *visama* ("uneven, contrary, wrong") or *vissagandha* ("smelling like raw meat," and so possibly "foul").

    Bhikkhu (the term for a Buddhist monk) is here translated as "mendicant" in order to convey the relationship between *bhikkhu* and the verbal root from which it derives, *bhikṣ*, "to beg," thus *bhikkhati*, "to beg."

268–269. The words "silence" (*monena*) and "one weighs" (*munāti*) play off the word for a sage, *muni* (literally, "silent one"). In ancient times a *muni* was someone who took a vow of silence as a form of religious practice.

271–272. "Ordinary people" (*puthujjana*). "Virtue or religious practice" (*sīlabbata*).

CHAPTER 20. THE PATH (MAGGA)

273–275. "Gods and humans" is a rendering of *dipadānaṃ* (two-footed beings). A more literal translation of the last line is "Having known (or experienced) the removal of the arrows."

276. *Tathāgata* is a title for a buddha. It is not clear what the word literally means; possibly it was meant to have several meanings. Buddhaghosa, perhaps the most important ancient commentator of the Theravada tradition, gives eight derivations for the word. In modern times *tathāgata* is often explained as a compound made up of two words: *tathā* ("thus") and either *gata* ("gone") or *āgata* ("come"). Because the term can be understood either way, it means either "the one thus gone" or the "the one thus come." In *Itivuttaka* 112, the Buddha suggests several other explanations of the title based on the word *tatha*.

277–279. Together, the first lines of each of these three verses are known as the "three characteristics (*tilakkhana*)." These three characteristics are often understood as the key insights of "insight meditation" (*vipassanā*). The first two characteristics are about created things (*saṅkhārā*), while the third is about all things (*dhammā*), that is, both created and uncreated things. "The uncreated," often translated as "the unconditioned," is a synonym for Nirvana. The third characteristic states that both Nirvana and created things cannot be identified with one's self. Since it is not possible to say that Nirvana is impermanent or that it has some inherent characteristic of suffering, the first two characteristics refer only to "created things."

   "Disenchanted" (*nibbida*).

280. "Path of insight" is a translation of *paññāya maggaṃ*; *paññā* usually is translated into English as "wisdom."

282. "Wisdom" (*bhūri*). "From [spiritual] practice" (*yogā*).

283. This verse seems to contain a number of word plays and so is difficult to translate. For example, it plays on the two

meanings of *vana,* "forest" and "desire." The commentaries explain that once, when the Buddha told his monks to cut down the *vana,* they started to clear the forest. He then had to clarify that he meant them to "cut down the forest of desire, not the forest of trees." One tradition takes the forest to refer to the gross defilements that have consequence in one's future lives, and the underbrush to refer to defilements that have consequence in one's current life. The verse also might be punning between *nibbanā* ("free of forest") and *nibbāna* ("Nirvana").

285. "Cultivate" (*brūhaya*). The Well-Gone-One (*Sugata*) is an epithet for the Buddha.

288. "Death" (*antekena;* literally, "end-maker").

CHAPTER 21: MISCELLANEOUS (PAKIṆṆAKA)

290. It is not clear how to translate *mattā* (here translated as "lesser"). It more literally seems to mean "measured" or "moderate." K. R. Norman believes the original meaning was "material things," and he translates it so (Norman, 1997, p. 43 and note 290).

294–295. The shock of the literal meaning of these verses adds force to whatever metaphoric message they carry. DhpA explains that "mother" refers to craving, "father" to conceit, the two warrior kings to metaphysical views of eternalism and annihilationism, the kingdom to the twelve sense spheres (*āyatana*), and the subjects of the kingdom to the passion for pleasure dependent on the sense spheres. "A tiger" is a translation of *veyyagghapañcamaṃ,* literally, "with a tiger as fifth" or "that of which its fifth element pertains to tigers." The DhpA commentary describes this as referring to either the five hindrances (sensual desire, ill will, sloth and torpor, restlessness and anxiety, and doubt) or just to the fifth hindrance, doubt. For a definition of *brahmin*, see the note to the title of chapter 26, below.

298. *Saṅgha* (assembly) refers to the monastic community and to the people who have attained one of the four stages of liberation.

301. *Bhāvanā*, here translated as "[spiritual] practice," literally means "cultivation" or "development" and is a common word for engaging in the practices taught by the Buddha, especially meditation practice.

302. The traditional commentary explains that "a traveler" is someone wandering through samsara.

CHAPTER 22. HELL (NIRAYA)

307. *Kāsāvakaṇṭhā*, here rendered as "who wear the saffron robe," literally means "yellow necks," that is, those who wear the yellow Buddhist robe around their necks or those whose necks are stained yellow from the dye contained in the monastic robes.

308. "The alms-food of the people" is a translation of *raṭṭhapiṇḍaṃ* (literally, "alms-food of the realm").

309–310. I have taken the liberty of translating *para dārā* as "the spouse of another." *Dārā* often means "wives" but may include any women under the protection of a man.

312. "Much fruit" (*mahapphalaṃ*, literally "great fruit").

313. Dust (*rajaṃ*) figuratively refers to greed, hate, and delusion.

316. "Bad rebirth" translates *duggatiṃ,* which more literally means "bad destination" or "bad existence."

Chapter 23. The Elephant (nāga)

322–323. "To that place not gone to" is a translation of *gaccheyya agataṃ disaṃ. Agataṃ disaṃ* is usually understood to mean *nibbāna* (Nirvana). Translating *agataṃ* as "not gone to" gives the double connotation of a place not yet reached and a place not reachable with any conventional ideas of going or progress.

324. The commentaries state that Dhanapālaka ("Guardian of the Wealth") was an elephant that, while being held in luxurious captivity by the king of Kasi, only longed to return to the forest to care for his mother.

325. The Pali for "is reborn again and again" literally says "comes into a womb again and again."

326. "Elephant keeper" (*aṇukusaggaho;* literally, "one who handles the goad (of an) elephant driver)."

329. DhpA explains that Matanga was an elephant who had had enough of the difficulties of living with a herd and so went off to enjoy a solitary life in the forest.

CHAPTER 24. CRAVING (TAṆHĀ)

334. "A creeping vine," literally, "a *māluvā* vine," which apparently strangles the trees it grows on. The simile thus refers to something that both spreads quickly and eventually kills its support. "Ever onward" is a translation of *hurāhuraṃ*. *Hurā* seems to mean "there" or "beyond." *Hurāhuraṃ* could perhaps be translated more literally as "onward and onward again." The expression is sometimes understood to mean "from existence to existence" or "from life to life."

335. Literally, "Like *bīraṇa* grass after rain." The *Pāli Text Society Dictionary* explains that *bīraṇa* is a fragrant grass with the Latin name *Andropogon muricatum*. It is possible that it is a fairly tall grass that grows quickly.

339. The commentarial tradition understands the "thirty-six streams" as referring to three forms of craving in relation to each of the six internal and the six external sense spheres (*āyatana;* see note to verses 1–2, p. 115). In the "Discourse on Turning the Wheel of the Dharma," recorded as the Buddha's first sermon, the three forms of craving are craving for sensual pleasure, craving for becoming or existence, and craving for nonbecoming or nonexistence.

344. One traditional interpretation understands "underbrush" and "forest" to be synonyms for craving.

345–347. "Go forth" refers to leaving the household life for that of a renunciant.

348. Literally, "Let go in front, let go behind, and let go in between." The DhpA explains that "in front" refers to the past,

"behind" refers to the future, and "in between" refers to the present.

350. "Cultivate a focus on what's unpleasant" is a translation of *asubham bhāvayati*. This refers to a traditional Buddhist practice of focusing on the unappealing or foul parts of the body as a means to reduce attachment for the body.

351–352. "In one's final body" refers to the idea that since people who are fully liberated will not be reborn again, their current physical body is the last body they will have.

353. This verse quotes the Buddha talking about himself. For the context of the quote, see *Majjhima Nikāya* 1.171 and *Vinaya* 1.8.

CHAPTER 25. THE BHIKKHU (BHIKKHU)

Often translated as "monk," *bhikkhu* could more literally be translated as "mendicant," as I have done in verses 365 and 366. I have sometimes translated it as "a monastic" so it can refer to monastics of any gender. The ancient Theravada commentaries state that anyone engaged in Buddhist meditation practice, whether man or woman, can be called a *bhikkhu*.

360–361. *Sādhu*, here translated as "good," can also mean "excellent, virtuous, profitable, meritorious."

363. "And illuminates the teaching and the goal" is a translation of *attham dhammam ca dīpeti*. Both *attham* ("goal, meaning, purpose, message") and *dhammam* have a range of

meanings, and probably no one English choice does either of them justice.

365. "Mendicant" (*bhikkhu*).

367. "Body-and-mind" (*nāma-rūpa*). See the note to verse 221.

370. The explanation for the three references to "five" given in brackets comes from DhpA. The lower fetters are (1) views pertaining to self or what belongs to self, (2) doubt, (3) grasping at precepts and practices, (4) sensual passion, and (5) ill will. The higher fetters are (1) attachment to phenomena of form, (2) attachment to the formless phenomena, (3) conceit, (4) restlessness, and (5) ignorance. The five faculties are faith, effort, mindfulness, concentration, and wisdom or insight.

372. "Insight" (*paññā*). "Meditative absorption" (*jhānaṃ*).

373. The DhpA commentary states that "an empty dwelling" refers to any solitary place.

374. *Khandhā*: the aggregates; see note to verse 202. "The Deathless": see note to verse 21.

378. "The world's bait" is a translation of *lokāmiso,* a compound word made up of *loka* ("world") and *āmiso. Āmiso* originally meant "raw meat." It came to have the additional meanings "of the flesh," "worldly," and "food." *Lokāmiso* could also be translated as "the physical/material world," "worldly gain," or "the object of worldly appetites."

CHAPTER 26. THE BRAHMIN (BRĀHMAṆA)

The brahmins were the members of the hereditary priestly class. In this chapter, however, the word *brāhmaṇa* is redefined to refer not to someone born into that class but rather to someone of worthy conduct and spiritual maturity.

384. "Tranquillity and insight" is an explanatory translation of *dvayesu dhammesu* (literally, "with two dharmas [practices]"). I have translated this expression according to the explanation for it given by the DhpA.

385. "Not-beyond" (*apāra*) is this world as opposed to the world beyond (*pāra;* literally, "the other [shore]").

388. The last two lines contain a wordplay between *pabbājeti* ("drives out, makes go away, banishes") and *pabbajati* ("goes forth into the renunciate life"). It is likely that there is an additional wordplay between *samacariyā* ("living peacefully") and *samaṇo* ("renunciant").

389. The addition of "anger" is based on the commentaries' explanation of this verse.

392. "The Fully Self-Awakened One" is a common epithet for the Buddha. He was "self-awakened" because he found the path to liberation on his own, without the help of another teacher. He was "fully self-awakened" because his liberation was complete.

396. This verse dismisses the traditional understanding that one became a brahmin by being born into a brahmin family. "Is called 'self-important'" translates *bhovādi nāma so hoti,* which

could be translated more literally as "he has the name '*bho-vādi.*'" A *bhovādi* is literally "someone who says *bho*" (a vocative interjection used to address someone of lower or equal status to oneself). Someone who uses this frequently is claiming a high status and is thus seen as filled with self-importance. Cf. *Sutta Nipāta* 620.

397. It has been proposed that *na paritassati,* here translated as "does not tremble," could be better translated as "does not feel any desire." The Chinese translations of the same term support this suggestion (Dhammajoti, p. 272).

398. According to DhpA, the strap refers to hatred, the thong to craving, the cord to the sixty-two wrong views (see *Brahmajala Sutta,* DN 1), the bridle to the latent tendencies, and the crossbar to ignorance.

400. See note to verses 351–352 for a definition of "final body."

404. What is here translated as "whoever is not mixed up with" could also be rendered "whoever does not associate with." "Renunciants" is literally "homeless ones" (*anāgārehi*).

405. *Tasesu thāvaresu,* here translated as "both timid and strong," might more literally be rendered as "frightened and firm," "moving and unmoving," or "perturbed and unperturbed."

406. "Whoever is unopposing among those who oppose" is a translation of *aviruddhaṃ viruddhesu.*

411. "Established in the Deathless" translates *amatogadhaṃ anuppattaṃ.* Different opinions exist whether *ogadhaṃ* is re-

lated to *ogathati,* "to plunge into," or to *ogadhati,* "to be established." The commentaries connect it to the former. Pali usage seems to indicate the latter. See Bhikkhu Bodhi, *The Connected Discourses of the Buddha* (Boston: Wisdom Publications, 2000), pp. 1093–1094, note 243.

413. "The delight for existence is extinct" is an attempt to translate the compound *nandībhavaparikkhīṇaṃ.* I am unsure how to understand this expression. It could possibly mean "whose delight and process of becoming are extinct," "whose existence based on delight is extinct," or "whose delight for further becoming is extinct." *Bhava,* the middle word in the compound, is often translated as "becoming" and sometimes as "existence" or "life." It refers to the active functioning of life that generates further existence or being.

414. *Nibbuta,* here translated as "released," has been rendered by other translators as "pacified," "attained Nibbāna," "has waned away," and "content." In choosing "released," I am relying on Thanissaro Bhikkhu's discussion of *nibbāna* in his work *Mind Like Fire Unbound* (Barre, Mass.: Dhamma Dana Publications, 1993).

415. "Passion for existence is extinct" (*kāmabhavaparikkhīṇaṃ*).

416. "Craving for existence is extinct" translates *taṇhābhavaparikkhīṇaṃ.* I am unsure how to translate this. Other possible translations are "whose existence based on craving is extinct" and "whose craving for becoming is extinct."

418. "Without attachments" (*nirūpadhi*). *Upadhi* can mean "attachment" as well as "substrate" or "basis" (for rebirth).

419. "Well-gone" (*sugataṃ*) refers to someone who is liberated.

420. *Gandhabba*s are heavenly musicians. "Toxins": see note to verse 89, p. 122.

421. "In front, behind, and in between" is a translation of *pure ca pacchā ca majjhe*. Sometimes this has been rendered into English as "past, future, and present." "Has nothing" (*akiñca-nam*); the word *kiñcanam*, meaning "anything," is sometimes understood to refer to the defilements. *Akiñcanam* could then mean "not having defilements."

Bibliography

Brough, John. *The Gāndhārī Dharmapada: Edited with an Introduction and Commentary.* London Oriental Series, vol. 7. London and New York: Oxford University Press, 1962.

Buddharakkhita, Thera Acharya. *The Dhammapada: The Buddha's Path of Wisdom.* (With an introduction by Bhikkhu Bodhi.) Kandy, Sri Lanka: Buddhist Publication Society, 1985. This translation is available online at www.access toinsight.org/canon/sutta/khuddaka/dhp/index.html.

Carter, John Ross, and Paliwadana, Mahinda. *The Dhammapada (A New English Translation with the Pali Text and the First English Translation of the Commentary's Explanations of the Verses with Notes Translated from Sinhala Sources and Critical Textual Comments).* Oxford and New York: Oxford University Press, 1987.

———. *The Dhammapada: The Sayings of the Buddha. Translated with an Introduction and Notes.* Oxford and New York: Oxford University Press, 2000. This contains the same translation of the *Dhammapada* as the previous reference. It does not have the translation of the traditional commentaries, but it does have a nice introduction absent in the earlier work.

BIBLIOGRAPHY

Dhammajoti, Bhikkhu Kuala Lumpur. *The Chinese Version of Dharmapada. Translated with Introduction and Annotations*. Colombo, Sri Lanka: University of Kelaniya, The Postgraduate Institute of Pali and Buddhist Studies, 1995.

Müller, F. Max. *The Dhammapada: A Collection of Verses, Being One of the Canonical Books of the Buddhists*. Sacred Books of the East, vol. 10, part 1. Oxford: Oxford University Press, 1924.

Nārada, Thera. *The Dhammapada: Pāli Text and Translation with Stories in Brief and Notes*. Calcutta: Maha Bodhi Society of India, 1978.

Norman, K. R. *The Word of the Doctrine (Dhammapada). Translated with an Introduction and Notes*. Pali Text Society Translation Series 46. Oxford: The Pali Text Society, 1997.

Thanissaro Bhikkhu (Geoffry DeGraff). *Dhammapada: A Translation*. Barre, Mass.: Dhamma Dana Publications, 1998. This translation is available online at www.access toinsight.org/canon/sutta/khuddaka/dhp1/index.html.

Appendix

CROSS-REFERENCE TO PARALLEL VERSES IN OTHER BUDDHIST TEXTS

THIS APPENDIX PROVIDES THE REFERENCES FOR *Dhammapada* verses that have parallel verses elsewhere in the Pali canon. References preceded by the abbreviation *cf.* ("compare") indicate passages that are similar enough to the Pali verses to be noteworthy. This concordance should not be taken as complete.

Names in italics refer to the speaker of the verse if other than the Buddha.

Abbreviations used:

AN	*Anguttara Nikāya*
DN	*Dīgha Nikāya*
Dhp	*Dhammapada*
It.	*Itivuttaka*
Jāt.	*Jātaka*
MN	*Majjhima Nikāya*
SN	*Saṃyutta Nikāya*
Sn.	*Sutta Nipāta*
Thag.	*Theragāthā*

Thig.   *Therīgāthā*
Vin.   *Vinaya Piṭaka*
Ud.   *Udāna*

2. Cf. Thag. 1041–43 (*Ven. Ānanda*).
3–5. Jāt. 3.488.
3–6. Vin 1,349; Jāt. 3.212.
3, 5–6. MN. 3.154.
6. Thag. 275 (*Ven. Sabhiya*); Thag. 498 (*Ven. Kaccāna*).
9–10. Thag. 969, 970 (*Ven. Phussa*); Jāt. 2.198, 5.50.
13–14. Thag. 133–134 (*Ven. Rādha*).
21. Jāt. 5.99.
23. Cf. SN 2.232.
26. SN 1.25 (*a deva*).
26–27. MN 2.105 (*Ven. Angulimāla*); Thag. 883–884 (*Ven. Angulimāla*).
28. DN 2.39 (*Brahmā*).
32. AN 2.40; It. 45.
42. Ud. 4.3.
47. Cf. Dhp 287.
49. Jāt. 1.349
51–52. Thag. 323–324 (*Ven. Subhūta*).
54. AN 1.226.
66–68. SN 1.57 (*deva Khema*).
69. Cf. SN 1.85.
76–77. Thag. 993–994 (*Ven. Sāriputta*).
80. MN 2.105 (*Ven. Angulimāla*); Thag. 877 (*Ven. Angulimāla*). Cf. Dhp 145.
81. Vin. 1.185; Thag. 643 (*Sona Kolivisa*).
85–89. SN 5.24; AN 5.232–33, 253–54.
87. Cf. Sn. 526.
93. Thag. 92 (*Ven. Vijaya*).

94. Thag. 205 (*Ven. Brahmāli*); cf. Thag. 206.

98. SN 1.233; Thag. 991 (*Ven. Sāriputta*).

99. Thag. 992 (*Ven. Sāriputta*).

109. Cf. Sn. 325.

119–120. Jāt. 1.231.

125. SN 1.13, 1.164; Sn. 662; Jāt. 3.203.

129. Cf. Sn. 705.

131–132. Ud. 2.3.

141. Cf. Sn. 249.

142. Cf. Sn. 35.

143. SN 1.7 (*a deva*).

145. Thag. 19 (*Ven. Kula*); cf. Dhp 80.

146. MN 2.64 (*Ven. Ratthapāla*); Thag. 769 (*Ven. Ratthapāla*); Thag. 1020 (*Ven. Ānanda*).

148. Cf. SN 1.97.

151. SN 1.71; Jāt. 5.483.

152. Thag. 1025 (*Ven. Ānanda*).

153–154. Thag. 183–84 (*Ven. Sivaka*).

163. Cf. Ud. 5.8.

170. Cf. SN 3.140 and Sn. 1119.

172. MN 2.104 (*Ven. Angulimāla*); Thag. 871 (*Ven. Angulimāla*).

173. MN 2.104 (*Ven. Angulimāla*); Thag. 872 (*Ven. Angulimāla*).

176. It. 25; cf. MN 1.415.

180. SN 1.107.

183–185. DN 2.49–50 (*the Buddha Vipassī*).

185. Ud. 4.6.

186. Thig. 487 (*Ven. Sumedhā*).

186–187. Jāt. 2.313.

188–192. Jāt. 1.97.

191. SN 2.185; It. 24; Thig. 186 (*Ven. Cālā*), 193 (*Ven.*

Upacāla), 310 (*Ven. Cāpa*); Thag. 321; Thag. 1259 (*Ven. Vangīsa*).

198. Cf. Thag. 276 (*Ven. Sabhiya*).

200. SN 1.114; Jāt. 6.55; cf. Jāt. 6.54.

201. SN 1.83.

204. MN 1.508–10.

205. Sn. 257.

210. Cf. Vin. 1.10.

218. Cf. Thig. 12 (*Ven. Dhammadinnā*).

221. SN 1.23; cf. SN 1.25.

223. Jāt. 2.4.

230. AN 2.8.

238. Cf. Thag. 412.

239. Sn. 962.

241–243. AN 4.195.

246–247. Cf. AN 3.205.

252. Cf. Jāt. 3.223.

266–267. SN 1.182.

273. Cf. MN 1.508.

277–279. Thag. 676–78 (*Ven. Añña-Kondañña*).

292–293. Thag. 635–36 (*Ven. Sona Kolivisa*).

305. Cf. Sn. 709.

306. Sn. 661; Ud. 4.8.

306–308. It. 48.

311–314. SN 1.49 (*deva Tāyana*); SN 1.49 (Buddha quoting *deva Tāyana*).

312. Thag. 277 (*Sabhiya*).

315. Thag. 1005 (*Ven. Sāriputta*); Thig. 5 (*Ven. Tissa*); cf. Thag. 653 and 403 (*Ven. Malunkyāputta*); cf. Sn. 333.

320. Cf. Ud. 4.7.

325. Thag. 17, 101.

326. Thag. 77 (*Ven. Hatthārohaputta*), 1130 (*Ven. Tālaputta*).

328–329. Sn. 45, 46.

328–330. MN 3.154; Vin. 1.350.

330. Cf. Vin. 1.353.

334–337. Thag. 399–402 (*Mālunkyāputta*).

339–340. Cf. Thag. 760, 761.

340. Sn. 1034.

345. Cf. Thag. 187 ("a compassionate spirit"); cf. Sn. 38.

345–346. SN 1.77; Jāt. 2.140.

353. MN 1.171; Vin. 1.8. Cf. Sn. 211 and SN 2.284.

361. SN 1.73.

362. Thag. 981.

363. Cf. Sn. 850 and Thag. 2 (*Kotthita the Great*); Jāt. 2.350.

364. It. 86; Thag. 1032 (*Ven. Ānanda*).

367. Sn. 950; cf. Sn. 861.

368. Cf. Thag. 11 (*Ven. Gavaccha the Less*) and 521 (*Ven. Bhūta*).

370. SN 1.3; Thag. 15 (*Ven. Kunda-Dhāna*) and 633 (*Ven. Sona Kolivisa*).

374. Cf. Thag. 23 (*Ven. Gosāla*).

379. Cf. Thag. 637 (*Ven. Sona Kolivisa*).

381. Thag. 11 (*Ven. Gavaccha the Less*).

382. MN 2.104 (*Ven. Angulimāla*); Thag. 873 (*Ven. Angulimāla*); cf. Thag. 203.

383. SN 1.49 (*deva Tāyana*).

387. SN 2.284; cf. SN 1.15.

388. Cf. Ud. 1.4.

394. Jāt. 1.481.

396–423. Sn. 620–47.

398. Cf. SN 1.16 and 1.63.

406. SN 1.236 (*the god Sakka*); Sn. 630.

414. Cf. AN 4.290.

421. Cf. Thag. 537 (*Ven. Ekavihāriya*).

423. Cf. MN 2.144; SN 1.167; AN 1.165; It. 99.

Dhammapada verses that have parallels in non-Buddhist Indian literature are reported in the following sources:

Davids, Caroline A. F. Rhys. *Dhammapada: Verses on Dhamma and Khuddaka-patha,* in *The Minor Anthologies of the Pali Canon,* part 1. Oxford: The Pāli Text Society, 1931.

Rau, Walter. "Berkmerkungen und nicht-buddhistische Sanskrit-Parallelen zum Pāli-Dhammapada," in *Jñānnamuktāvali. Commemoration Volume in Honour of Johannes Nobel, on the Occasion of His 70*[th] *Birthday Offered by Pupils and Colleagues.* New Delhi: International Academy of Indian Culture, 1959, pp. 159–75.

Bollée, Willem B. *Reverse Index of the Dhammapada, Suttanipāta, Thera- and Therīgāthā Pādas with Parallels from the Āyāranga, Sūyagada, Uttarajjhāyā, Dasaveyāliya and Isibhāsiyāim.* Studien zur Indologie und Iranistik 8. Reinbek: Inge Wezler, 1983.

Hinüber, Oskar von, and K. R. Norman, ed. *Dhammapada.* Oxford: Pāli Text Society, 1994.